Praise for *Shattered Paradise*

"From the tropical memories in Ileana Araguti's *"Shattered Paradise: Memoirs of a Nicaraguan War Child"* flows tropical memories mixed with feelings of failures and promises. Her story is captivating, even riveting, within the best testimonio tradition: quite an accomplishment for her first book."

—Francisco A. Lomelí, Professor, UCSB

"In her lyrical memoir, Ileana Araguti honors her native land in all of its beauty and conflicts with the kind of loving honesty every homeland deserves. *Shattered Paradise* is one of the most moving memoirs I've read."

—Bruce McAllister, author of *The Village Sang to the Sea: A Memoir of Magic*

"The author has delivered a well-written, moving manuscript. She has a strong talent for writing in a way that readers can "see" the scenes she paints. I congratulate her."

—Jim Dobkins, author and co-author of eleven books

D1457632

SHATTERED PARADISE

Memoirs of a
Nicaraguan
War Child

ILEANA ARAGUTI

New Trends Press
California

Shattered Paradise
A New Trends Press Book

Ileana Araguti

Copyright © 2013 Ileana Araguti

Website: www.newtrendspress.com

Published by:

New Trends Press
An imprint of Joseph Gutiz Publishing
PO Box 493, Moreno Valley, CA 92556

Print - ISBN: 978-0-9884025-3-9

AUTHOR'S NOTE: My childhood memoirs wish to exalt the beauty and miracle of life, not the mischief of war and human greed. I aim to recreate events as they occurred and were retold by family and friends, mending along the way mental lapses or any creative stimuli that might get in the way. Some characters have been renamed, not to preserve their innocence nor their guilt, but rather their inner intentions.

Ox that I saw in my childhood, as you steamed
in the burning gold of the Nicaraguan sun,
there on the rich plantation filled with tropical
harmonies; woodland dove, of the woods that sang
with the sound of the wind, of axes, of birds and wild bulls:
I salute you both: you are both my life.

You, heavy ox, evoke the gentle dawn
that signaled it was time to milk the cow,
when my existence was all white and rose;
and you, sweet mountain dove, cooing and calling,
you signify all that my own springtime, now
so far away, possessed of the Divine Springtime.

Far Away
Rubén Darío

Dedicated to those
who drive my spirit. . .

Amanda, my oldest sister, your life was short—perhaps a blessing. Socorro, the second oldest, you helped others selflessly and struggled until your end with the greatest dignity. Juan Carlos, the strong-hearted one, you escaped many times, but returned only to die again. My maternal grandparents, you are my childhood's best memories. I've always known you are watching from above.   The remaining members of my family: Mama, you made a painful choice and allowed me the privilege of freedom and healing, I ADMIRE and LOVE YOU. Papa, you taught me inner strength. Francisca, Ramón and Francisco—distance has only made our bond stronger, I admire your resilience. Benjamin, the second youngest before me, more than my brother you are also my best friend. My husband, daughter and son, you are my laughter and ultimate inspiration. To all who share the unity only love and suffering could bring. Your inner strength keeps you alive and guides you through the labyrinths of life—never give in to the passing perils of life. Last but not least, the high-spirited Nicaraguans, you deserve your own—

Divine Springtime: A fruitful and peaceful land.

CONTENTS

SHATTERED

PARADISE

Prologue

To the Sound of Für Elise and the Ave María

FÜR ELISE—not a mere bagatelle. If you listen to it long enough, simple yet profound, you could almost feel time pausing momentarily. If a selection of music with melodies of heroism and despair along with a strange sense of both happiness and melancholy were to describe my childhood, Für Elise by Beethoven would surely be the one. The universal piano piece became a catalyst and inspiration in my younger life amid the poetic revolutionary war in Nicaragua, which began in 1972. Für Elise would be one of the melodies other than the *Ave María* that resonated through Mama's old record player and at times through the speakers of the town's church, to announce the merciless toll of the hour.

In my early and exhilarating years, I learned to ride a horse to its utmost potential through the whimsical cloud and rain forests, tell a white lie, and suck on sun-ripened red coffee beans—without becoming overly excited and without swallowing the seeds, for if I swallowed the seeds, a tree might grow inside my body. At least that's how Mama would instill fear in me, hoping I would stop sucking on those delectable coffee beans. And as the seasons changed I learned many things, yet the milestone moment that accelerated my growth would be the shattering of my paradise, through the slow passage of time—where every tick of the minute lasted its actual sixty seconds.

Although barely the size of New York State, Nicaragua is the largest country in Central America, dwarfing its neighbors Costa Rica and Honduras. The biggest rain forest in Central America lies within its borders, hydrated by tropical and subtropical humidity and ten months of rainfall. Once the richest in wealth and natural resources, Nicaragua is now the poorest country in Central America and perhaps in the Western Hemisphere. Note: It is the poorest only by means of paucity of wealth and diminishing natural resources—never by the lack of human spirit. A Nicaraguan could be rich or poor, but mainly poor—not much in between. He or she weighs wealth by jokes told in the wake of a siesta, bedtime stories that amuse, poems recited before execution and mainly by how many dreams are held onto—however faint these might become. Nicaraguans are known to push forward until their veins have dried out. Our main weakness: the curse of an elephant's memory—the type that never forgets.

I never forget where I come from—believe me, there were times I've tried. Twenty-four years have passed since I left my native country of Nicaragua. I come from "the land of lakes and volcanoes," as many refer to it. And because of the oceans that surround it, hurricanes and tsunamis could strike it at any time. My ancestors that knew better—settled where the soil appeared richer and away from the threat of the most menacing natural disasters. Little did they know that the land of their dream would gain a reputation as one of the most war-torn regions in the country. Yet after a while, and like the others, they too resigned to their fate. They figured they would die of something anyhow, and instead settled deeper into the refuge of the northern highlands of the forests. No doubt, it was a beautiful place, if only they had kept us children away from playing in its surroundings—a tantalizing trap of exotic flora and extraordinary fauna.

My life began with a beautifully landscaped childhood but later transformed into a story of survival and quick adaptations, amid a cloud forest and a tiny Spanish colonial town, so distant that hardly anyone knew it existed. It was an ordinary life, lived with unfailing rooted beliefs—Roman Catholic ones, intertwined along the way with folktales and a colorful imagination—until the revolutionary war, one of the bloodiest wars recorded in the history of Nicaragua. A poetic war I only survived thanks to Mama's unrelenting prayers and the guidance of the provincial priests, the Spanish missionary teachers who brought along their subduing classical music—my bridge to memories, and of course the naïveté of childhood, particularly that of a Nicaraguan girl raised by a weeping mother, a womanizer father, unyielding school nuns, and a tantalizing landscape filled with landmines and grenades camouflaged between the canopies of cloud forests and humid soil that were left first by the conquistadores, the cursed dictatorship and the dynasty of the Somoza family for over four decades from 1936 to 1979, as well as the special interests of foreign governments: the United States from 1912 to 1933, the Soviet Union, Cuba and ultimately the 1979 U.S. aided Contra revolutionary fight against the intermittent Sandinista government.

The history of Nicaragua is an evolving diary, written by poets and martyrs, for every second that passes by, a story from the past reveals: "Papa, look at this rock!" A child had once said when the innocent dug up a grenade. A landowner had surrendered his land while leaving his ox behind to serve as meat to the hungry soldiers. A loaded rifle had been given to a young boy before he reached puberty, but frightened, he pointed it towards the wrong direction and shot his own foot. Nonetheless, the young soldier left to battle, simply hoping for a poem to be composed on behalf of his bravery—or perhaps at the very least, he could become a martyr—another immortal face painted on the humid Nicaraguan walls.

I was born in the city of Jinotega, a speck on the map then. It is also known as the City of Mist because of the dense fog that continuously embraces the valley. It is a place heavily influenced by Franciscan Friars and the Spanish Missionaries, whose sole mission would be to convert our souls through christening and the Holy Catholic Eucharist. It was through their teachings that I learned to recite a particular Spanish prayer presumed to prevent any evil from coming my way:

Que fuerte venís, mas fuerte
es mi Dios. La santisima
Trinidad me libre de vos.

The prayer claims that although evil might come forth strongly, God and the Holy Trinity would save me from all evil.

"Close your eyes, Ileana, and repeat the prayer three times whenever you're in danger," Mama often counseled.

*Que fuerte venís...*I repeated often, and more than three times, until one day I failed to close my eyes, and as a result, my tongue froze in time. Mama must have forgotten to explain that if God did not respond to the prayer at any given moment, then I needed to run away!

1

Guardian Angel

CITY OF MIST, 1978. The irony of life: a game of chess guided by predictions, choices—the element of time. What makes us interesting beings is the ability to go through life unnoticed, to blend amongst the ordinary and the grand, and to camouflage a past to where no one can tell it ever existed. But at the end of the day, we return to who we once were and still are—keepers of memories. I grew up commemorating my oldest and deceased sister's birthday, until the age of five. *"Apúrense,"* Mama bleated, urging us to hurry. Appearing never to age, she guided her thin silhouette throughout the house, rejoicing on the few happy memories that still floated in her mind. Still, amid her distracted mind, Mama found time to come into my room to

18

inspect the status of my hair. Our young helper Tatiana had just finished irritating my scalp with a wide-toothed comb when Mama came in. Frail in appearance but still strong, Mama removed the comb from Tatiana's hand and with rushed strokes nearly combed all of the cuticles out of my head until my rebellious hair came to an acceptable submission. "She's ready!" Tatiana would then announce, as once again we witnessed the reflection on the mirror exposing a random teardrop sliding down Mama's cheek as she smoothed rose balm onto her heart-shaped lips. Every year since Amanda passed away, the ritual remained the same. We attended mass and celebrated my long-deceased sister's birthday, in the same way we celebrated our own.

A final mass offered for Amanda would take place at my maternal grandparents' hometown, as it was there that the first mass took place. We traveled from the City of Mist on the dusty and pot-holed dirt road to the colonial province of San Rafael Del Norte for what felt like an eternity. Then upon our arrival, inside the historical cathedral of the sleepy town, a tall and longhaired man, whose nearly naked body hung in agony over a heavy cross, welcomed us. His bloody face covered by thorns, broken skin and relentless stare reminded everyone of his loving sacrifice and of the need for repentance to absolve our sins. As the Holy Mass progressed, the fervent crowd barely paid attention to the humble priest, the Franciscan Friar Odorico

D'Andrea, who is now in the process of canonization to become the town's future saint. Mama had requested the priest to perform this ceremony, as it would be a memorable one. It was father Odorico who had first celebrated the mass on behalf of Amanda's passing away and now Mama wished for this last mass to be concluded in the same place and with the same priest. But soon after the penitential rite, father Odorico shouted nearly in despair, "NOW IS THE TIME TO REPENT, reflect on your sins, and REPENT at once!" Mama turned to Papa, but he quickly turned away irritated by her reproachful stare, the priest's condemnation and the strong odor of incense. Father Odorico knew his role; his sole mission since he arrived at San Rafael Del Norte would be to save the souls of its people. He even wrote a letter to Papa asking him to correct his womanizing wrongdoings, but Papa simply ignored his warnings.

"A brave man carries a strong soul," the priest added while proceeding with the homily.

Silky white curtains and fragrant roses decorated the supreme pillars of the old cathedral and revived the moments of a time lost once again. After the mass, I walked along with my six rambunctious siblings back to our Abuelos' home, slowly on the stone road that was gradually turning into gravel, followed by a few guests. Once there, guests helped themselves to warm food and coffee. Inside the Abuelos' home, in a corner decorated with fresh cut flowers, long white candles, and a white embroidered tablecloth, remained an old photograph of a child, protected by an equally old brass frame. Customary with most of our celebrations, Mama led prayers of grace, while Papa scolded us children out to play. And while inhaling and exhaling their cigars, men encircled Papa and exchanged provincial rumors. Outside, we children played games and stuck the tail to a paper donkey nailed to a tree. My brother Benjamin and I took our turn last as we became sidetracked by listening to the grownups' conversations. Mama and the other women exchanged stories from the past; Papa faced the horizon, somber and inattentive with an empty gaze while the other men encircled him into their conversations. And a few minutes later, a tail was in my hand.

"Almost," Benjamin shouted as I approached the paper donkey.

"To your right," another child said.

"No, to the left," Benjamin insisted.

I laughed as I soon discovered that I had placed the tail on the donkey's nose. Meanwhile, glancing at Papa, I could not help but wonder about his absent stare, and Mama's obsessive prayers. We entered the house again only to indulge in sweet corn rosquilla bread, which we would dip into a warm cup of freshly brewed *café con leche*. Then I quickly escaped outside again before the women would ask us to sing following the prayers. I ended up at last under a tree from where we continued to observe Papa's constant lack of engagement with the life around him. Curious about my distinctive family tradition, Dulce, a neighborhood friend, asked a question that had often boggled people's minds.

"Do your parents always celebrate your sister's birthday in this way every year?"

There is a story about it. I sighed, recalling how I had listened to it for the first time while Abuelo Lalo folded roasted tobacco leaves.

- - - - - -

"Life has many turns, *mi niña*," Abuelo would say, as he dried up the tears that poured out of my eyes.

My parents had argued again. It had been a couple of weeks since Papa had gone to seek the refuge of his mountains. Abuelo spoke calmly, while folding roasted tobacco leaves for Abuela with his long and gentle fingers onto small pieces of wax paper, folding every piece with utmost precision, until each end would seal with perfect symmetry, as if scared to unfold to the fury of its master. Abuelo no longer smoked but enjoyed crafting the cigars for Abuela. He stopped smoking after a horse threw him against a gate and he suffered a chest injury. After his accident, he asked Virgin Mary for a miracle in exchange for stopping smoking. The miracle was granted, his chest healed and Abuelo never smoked again. Abuelo was a master storyteller, and on that day he decided it was time for me to hear a story from the past, one he felt I was ready to comprehend. And while rolling, folding and adding to the growing pyramid of cigars, he began to rekindle moments of our past as Abuela slowly inhaled and exhaled her newly wrapped cigar. The more he said, the more I understood that no one comes to life without a purposeful destiny.

According to my beloved Abuelo, my parents' marriage began with a promise of love, which made my young Mama agree to all ideas Papa proposed. She followed as a child follows a parent—right behind, no questions asked. Then one day, deep into the cloud forest of Nicaragua, fear thickened the air, and the warm soil's vapors permeated through the wild grass. The torrential storm unleashed its fury, over-flooding riverbanks, and creating new paths along the way. Lightning parted the skies covered by an ominous curtain of clouds, which in turn brought unusually cold air upon my parents' isolated farmhouse. The reason for such wrath remains unclear. Papa had blamed it on natural disasters, possibly a hurricane or the exploitation of the land's resources: the chained monkeys, deforestation and the extracting of scarlet macaws from their nests. Mama had blamed the Lord for washing away our sins, and I only blamed the unremitting tears escaping Mama's soul at the recollection of an event, one that had happened so long ago.

For many years, I remained uncertain of what made Mama passionate for Papa. Out of respect to my parents, I never asked. Perhaps it was his deep cleft chin, his light brown hair, his right cheek dimple or his incurable obstinacy. His height could not have attracted her, for Mama always stood taller than Papa. This disproportion, often exaggerated by her high-heeled shoes, did not trouble Papa as long as her arm went under his, and he was close to her brunette hair and to her slim silhouette wrapped in porcelain skin.

"Follow me to the farm. I have built us a new home. I will hire helpers to help us plow the land. There, you will have everything, from organic foods to my unconditional love," Papa persuaded Mama.

"Wait until our first child is born," Mama responded. Papa could hardly wait to have her by his side, and solely for him. Therefore, just a month after the birth of their first child Amanda, he persuaded her to follow him to their remote farm amid the forest. He wished to build his family with only the symphony of the surrounding wildlife and the solemn company of the broadleaf trees.

"No! Wait at least one year before taking the child to the forest," Mama's unfailing priest, Father Odorico, advised.

"But father, the Holy Scripture commands that a good wife must accompany her husband wherever he might go! Please father, offer me your blessing."

"In the name of the Father, the Son and the Holy Spirit…" the humble priest blessed, exposing a re-sewn cassock beneath his armpit.

Mama packed an old leather bag that had belonged to Abuela and hurried to *La Estación* with little Amanda in her arms, wrapped snuggly in a pink blanket. Once there, she would ride the bus to meet her young husband by the roadside. The noise of the busy transit made little Amanda cry but Mama cradled her onto her warm chest. "It's all right my angel, we are going with Papa," she whispered to the child as her eyes glistened with emotions, typical of a woman in love.

The old yellow bus quickly overfilled its capacity with passengers who smelled like days-old fermentation. They were mostly *campesinos*, humble peasants traveling with live chickens tied up by their feet with a nylon string, upside down and hung onto wooden poles, which they carried over their shoulders nearly poking Mama on the head. Holding her breath behind her polite smile, she managed to shove herself to the very back of the bus where a gentleman would offer his own seat. The heavily pot-holed dirt road made her body ache, but she knew the pain was worth enduring, for beyond the dust clouds raised by the old diesel bus awaited a completely new world.

"Soon, our lungs will breathe fresh air; our eyes will see beautiful wild flowers, moss and exotic animals," she whispered again into the infant's ear. Throughout the journey, Mama drifted into a world of spectacular dreams. She imagined herself galloping along with little Amanda and her husband through the mystical cloud forests, bathing under cool waterfalls and dancing in a garden filled with scented wild orchids and melodious Toucanets. Suddenly the bus came to a sudden stop and Mama had to shove herself once more through the overly crowded bus, evading the flutter of the restless upside-down chickens on the campesinos' wooden poles.

Upon arrival, she found that Papa was waiting for them. He wore black high-water boots and a large cowboy hat. When Mama first saw him, her heart nearly exited off her chest and she felt butterflies inside her stomach. She nearly forgot she was carrying little Amanda. Papa waved by the roadside, exposing his deep cheek dimples and cleft chin as he held two horses firmly, a black Andalusia horse that was his and a red Clydesdale he had purchased for Mama. The young lovers hugged and without much hesitation, saddled onto their horses and embarked on a journey that would soon transform their lives forever. Papa held the reigns of her horse as they crossed the river that separated the road from the wilderness. The power of the river and the glimmer of its crystalline waters, along with the exotic surroundings of the forest embraced her. The perfume of vibrant wild flowers and humid soil aroused her senses. On her way to the remote farm, she even spied a resplendent quetzal in one of the tallest trees, its feathers a glory of iridescent hues.

Her joyous sighting reaffirmed she had made the right decision, for the Nicaraguan misty forest could lure any exotic species into its habitat: anteaters, howler monkeys, jaguars, three-toed sloths, flying snakes, poisonous frogs, and critters of all types.

"There!" Papa pointed to a small farmhouse, sheltered in isolation amid the dense forest. The solemnity of the landscape gave Mama an instant chill as slow and dense fog covered the sky.

"How far is the nearest neighbor?" she asked.

"Far enough not to disturb," he responded.

As the days passed, Mama adapted rapidly to the hustle of the farm life. She worked side-by-side with Papa milking the only cow he had received as a gift from his oldest brother Polín, and collecting warm eggs from the chickens' nests. They lived happily for over five months under the spell of the mystic forests, their blessings multiplying rapidly as their only cow would soon give birth to a calf. Papa's fertile land would produce enough crops for him to sell and expand his land into vast grasslands. Their first-born Amanda grew as beautiful as they dreamt her to be. She inherited the hazel eyes and light brown hair of her Papa, and day after day she enchanted his heart with soft cooing sounds.

One day a torrential downpour fell onto the weathered aluminum roof, its pounding making it impossible to sleep. However, no one tried to sleep that night. Mama had been up for nearly two nights, waiting for the first light of the morning to peek through the cracks of the wooden walls. Her eyes had become swollen and dim, her stomach empty and her nerves frayed. Amanda, my oldest sister and only six months old, was diagnosed with the Wicked Eye Disease by a well-known healer from the forest known as *El Curandero.*

"Su cría tiene mal de ojo," the wizened gray-haired *Curandero* said to Mama, claiming she had an illness an infant caught from adults when they stared into the newborn's eyes with envy or some type of physical agitation.

"Ah, I'm not in the mood for myths," Mama sighed.

"No, Doña Nena. Beautiful angels like this child are envied. Who has seen her lately?" *El Curandero* questioned.

"The last one to see her was Doña Domitila, the old lady that lives by the river. A kind soul, she brought us a head of red bananas. I made sure she held the baby right away!"

"Then, she was not it. Think harder," the old man insisted.

"Before Doña Domitila, Yervamala visited. Now that I think about it, she came storming into the room, straight to the baby and left in haste without holding her. Nonsense!"

"This baby needs a cleaning from evil," the old man suggested, while staring deep into the infant's eyes, as if seeing directly into her soul.

Accepting that she had no other choice and given the seriousness of the affliction and the isolation of the place, she allowed the old man to practice his mythical cures. The old Curandero was well known for healing the natives and assured Mama that Amanda's fever would soon cease. He proceeded to pull out a bottle of locally made *Cususa*, a native liquor out of an old nylon sack, opened it with his wrinkled and sun-dried hands, placed the bottle inside his mouth, took a big sip and warmed it inside as if rinsing his mouth. He then blew the warm liquor forcefully out of his mouth and onto Amanda's little body, revealing a few rotten and missing teeth. But realizing that the medicinal liquor had no effect, he then determined that it was not the Wicked Eye disease that afflicted the infant. Amanda's fever did not break; instead, it ravaged her little body more. Nonetheless, the elder curandero proceeded to stir yet another of his herbal concoctions, using only medicines from the surrounding forest. Steaming *salvia*, *yerbabuena* and other wild herbs in a tin can, he fed drops of the concoction into Amanda's mouth and later made his second diagnosis: she had a severe stomach infection called *Tifoidea*.

The old man then waited fervently beside the infant's wooden crib for the concoction to travel into her body, while scaring away the shadows of death he believed encircled the child with a leafy branch. Meanwhile distressed Mama's fingers traveled from one pearly rosary bead to the next. Mama's endless prayers, rosaries and novenas only calmed her spirit, as her sweet Amanda weakened by the minute. Eventually, unable to heal my oldest sister, the old curandero left the helpless child in the hands of God and my despairing Mama. Soon after the curandero left, Mama called out to one of the farm workers sitting outside the house. Pancho, who had been sitting outside chewing on sweet sugar cane, rushed into the house, unaware of his muddy boots. He held his hat politely over his chest as Mama, with a fainting voice and relentless tears, explained Amanda's critical state.

"Go on and call my husband. My baby needs real medicine and can't remain here," she instructed. Nodding once and spitting out the last piece of sugar cane, Pancho ran out of the house, mounted his horse and went to seek Papa who had gone to rescue the newborn calf, which had become stuck in the mud. Amanda and Mama waited for Papa's arrival, feeling powerless in the unremitting rain. Mama became frantic waiting for him to take Amanda to the nearest town of San Rafael Del Norte. However, Papa had to spend too much time rescuing the newborn calf and by now, it was too late to travel. The storm darkened the sky with greater fury and the child's weakened body became too frail to withstand the bumpy horse ride. In the end, all a distressed Mama could do was feed more wood to the fire and sit back in an old wooden rocking chair she had used daily to rock Amanda to sleep. The tears that escaped her soul competed with the incessant rain as she held onto a nearly lifeless child. Rocking back and forth, Mama comforted her sweet baby while singing a Spanish Lullaby in time with the creaking of the rocker.

Dormité mi niña,	*Go to sleep my child,*
dormité mi amor,	*go to sleep my love,*
dormité pedaso	*go to sleep little*
de mi corazón	*piece of my heart.*

Eventually Pancho located Papa and brought him home to Amanda. When Papa arrived, he stepped into the room slowly, leaving trails of water drops from his still wet boots and raincoat. His light steps swirled with emotions of fear and helplessness as he hoped that Amanda was simply going to sleep as she had done during the other one hundred and seventy nights of her life.

"The calf couldn't be saved," Papa announced as he hung his soiled coat on a rusted nail sticking out of the wooden wall. Tears rolled down Mama's cheeks while she gave Papa a stare that tattooed the deepest part of his heart.

"Hurry, come close," she wept. Amanda fought death for several hours: her eyes closed and opened, but she no longer cried. Her body became soft with dehydration, as if her skin no longer held onto her bones. Yet, for whatever reason, she remained alive.

"Here, *mi niña!*" Papa called to the infant, tickling her gently while attempting to play peek-a-boo. Amanda simply gazed back—too frail to react. While he held her gently in his arms, Amanda's eyes locked into his, as she forced a tender smile.

"*Mi niña* smiled!" Papa called to Mama.

Mama hurried to see. For a moment, hope filled their hearts, but the rain kept pouring, the thunder became louder, and Papa felt helpless as the life of his little angel vanished through his very own fingertips. His body shivered as though lightning had struck him; his heart was pulverized with pain, and his mind splintered with her passing away. He hugged little Amanda tightly and with a trembling hand managed to bless her with the sign of the cross, until she breathed for the last time. Her beautiful eyes dimmed as her body became cold and she left my parents forever.

The room became sepulchral as a deep and hollow sorrow chilled my parents' souls. Approaching Papa with light steps as if floating in the air, Mama reached out to him while he sobbed in disbelief. Holding Amanda's body tightly, he looked at her with the same haze-colored eyes that she had. Mama removed the still warm child from his arms, held her close to her heart, while bathing her little body with her own tears. Unable to bring Amanda back to life, Mama then resumed her previous position on the old wooden rocking chair, rocking and rocking, gently back and forth until stillness took over the room. She then sat steady and impassive as a stone. Papa stood still facing the cracks in the wooden wall briefly and then flung himself outside and mounted his horse again. A few minutes later, as witnesses would recount, screams were heard as they echoed through the storm. In his grief, Papa temporarily forgot Mama. And upon his return, two hours later, just as he had left her, Mama sat with Amanda cold in her arms. He stood by the door with shadows in his sunken eyes and feeling ill with a broken heart. "Pancho, hurry to San Rafael Del Norte and bring my mother-in-law," Papa instructed. The loyal man mounted his horse again and disappeared into the storm like a ghost, his raincoat fluttering out into the air. Abuela arrived nearly at sunrise alongside Pancho and Abuelo, wearing a dress and a poncho. She promptly dropped her bag onto the moist, pressed dirt floor and ran to Mama. She then consoled Mama whispering into her ear, as if not to awake the newborn, "She will be okay my sweet child." Noticing the nonresponsive glare of Mama, Abuela then gradually removed Amanda from her arms. She brought the dead child up to her hunched chest and wrapped her carefully with a pink baby blanket, giving sweet Amanda one final prayer and a kiss. The Abuelos, Papa and Mama, who carried the lifeless baby, rode their horses to *La Estación*, where a vehicle waited to take them to the town of San Rafael Del Norte. Abuelo said, and Mama later confirmed, that there were no words spoken: only a sad story permeated in the silence.

Upon their arrival at the town, long white candles welcomed little Amanda, as family and friends prayed Novenas after Novenas, sipping on freshly brewed coffee and savoring on warm corn rosquilla bread. Everyone wore white. The color represented the purity of a child, although black typically represented death and the dark clouds that covered their grieving hearts. The humble brick house in the small province welcomed the infant with white curtains hung from its wooden windows and the main door. Mama retreated to her mother's room soon after arriving, ignoring the guests.

"No one knows what inspired her spirit," Abuelo continued to tell.

She reappeared a few moments later and began to chant exalting songs, all in Amanda's name, causing convulsion in the crowd. Many thought sorrowfully that my poor Mama had lost her mind. But elegantly and loaded with dignity, she sat next to her small child's box and told Papa that her baby was now an angel in heaven. Her purity, as white as that of angels, needed to be honored. Father Odorico often preached that the death of a child is to be celebrated, as the child becomes another angel in heaven. He often played music through the large speakers of his church to celebrate a child's entrance into the gates of heaven. But staring blankly at the box of his beloved baby girl, Papa wore his usual blue jeans and white-cotton guayabera shirt, as he kept silent in the company of his own grief and the loud sound of the music Father Odorico's church played to celebrate the new birth of the child. The Ave María song, among a few others, was one that could be heard all the way to the cemetery.

"That is why we celebrate Amanda's birthday, year after year. She is our angel in heaven," Abuelo concluded.

After that night of discovery, after Abuelo retold the story of how my parents began to drift away from each other, I also began to understand many things: Mama's unrelenting prayers, over-sheltering of her children and unquestioned devotion towards Papa. As Amanda's birthday party concluded and all the guests headed back to their homes, we were left behind in our newly built Oakwood home that resembled my parents' farmhouse amid the forests, with only the distant memories that were told of a long gone sister. Upon the exit of the last guest, Mama gathered us together in a secretive and nearly chilling tone. She hugged and kissed all seven children on our foreheads, and announced that she was ready to let Amanda rest in peace. I felt confused, as I had figured she was already resting. From that day, we no longer celebrated Amanda's birthday, although we would never forget her or the day.

As many stories tend to tell, sometimes there is a reason to blame the route a person takes in life. Whether it is for good or bad, it exists. For Papa, who had never been faithful, the death of Amanda, his first child, intensified his womanizing antics and as a result, he chose that path for good. Amanda's farewell marked a new beginning for Mama and Papa; it was a tragic one. Perhaps it was the deep lesion carved onto the hearts of the newlyweds, or simply destiny that plays the usual tricks that befall some at one time or another. Personal heartache shadowed their love life. One small turn, one tragedy, or a simple choice can take anyone into unknown circumstances. My parents' marriage fell into a dark tunnel. People often said in an effort to console Mama that Amanda had become an advocate sitting by the throne of our Divinity, and as a result, our lives would be much better. Amanda, a new angel in heaven, according to the Holy Scriptures, would plead for our souls before our one God Jesus Christ—for the upcoming years of purgatory that awaited us here on earth. Every time Mama spoke of her sweet Amanda, she reminded us that the child was now in a better place and that she would never feel sorrow, emptiness, or pain of any kind, much less be conscious of the short transit of life on earth. Amanda, now in heaven and next to God, looks after each of us, as our very special Guardian Angel.

Since that tragedy, Papa refused to retreat from the fragrant forests completely. He became particularly rooted to the rich soil, the majestic shelter of the broadleaf trees, the mild canopy, the misty breeze of the whisky clouds and the sweet smelling orchids. He did everything in his power to save and retain this land and, as a result, turned weak to the spell of opportunistic mistresses whose lives were intertwined with the myths of the forests: the cries of the bewitched woman in the river, the wives of the headless rider and the brewers of heavenly and enticing potions, who would offer to work for him, in exchange for shelter and Mama's jealousy. Although Mama often claimed Papa had reasons to behave the way he did, for Amanda took part of his spirit with him, I often wondered if this was what Abuelo meant when he said, "*Mi niña*, there are several ways to kill a man."

2

Procreation Must Go On

FOR IT WAS God's will that I be born. I grew up in what appeared to be a happy home of ten: four rambunctious brothers, two beautiful sisters, our guardian angel Amanda in heaven, my parents and ME. Alternating between the town and the farm life during my siblings' academic years, my parents' time together dwindled. Papa, a chronic man of the land, did not care if we set aside our education to help him with the cultivation of the land and the herding of the cattle every morning by 5:00 a.m. Mama, a dedicated teacher who taught Papa how to read and calculate, often disagreed with what she called, "Papa's burro way of thinking." To her, education would not be an option but a necessity. Therefore, we were destined to alternate between the restricted small town life and the free escape of the natural world.

Following Amanda's death, Papa set out to purchase a permanent place in the City of Mist. The new house stood supported by wooden planks, an oversized wooden patio and large glass windows draped with curtains that seemed to contain springtime in their colors. Therefore, hoping to appease Mama's nerves after the loss of Amanda, Papa searched for the perfect new home for their rapidly growing family. After their fourth child Ramón, he was determined to purchase a house from a neighbor who custom built it for his wife. The rustic look, the location, and the large lot appealed to Papa so much that he offered a compelling amount of money to the owner, money he made through selling his best cattle to the slaughterhouse. The man's significant other became upset over the sale. Consequently, as restitution to Papa, the woman came to the decision of chopping up every living plant in the garden with a machete, making the house appear truly rustic for my parents to enjoy. Excited over the acquisition, Papa blindfolded Mama as they approached the new house and procceded holding hands, at times still resembling newlyweds. But upon arrival, Papa paused and sighed deeply.

"Here we are," he announced, no longer excited at the sight of the destruction. "Sick woman," he cursed while kicking up the dirt.

"Who are you calling a sick woman?" Mama mumbled, pulling off her blindfold with disdain.

"Not you; I meant the insane wife of the man who sold me this place. There is nothing worse than an ill-minded woman."

"You said it was a beautiful house with a fine-looking garden. This is a calamity!" Mama goaded.

"It was, when I bought it, but the man's wife lost her mind," he explained. "You could rebuild your own garden to your liking; the house is still striking, don't you agree?"

"The egg already hatched! It'll do," she accepted.

According to Abuela, it took only a few months for Mama to grow one of the best gardens in town. With a fabulous array of fragrant roses, red and white hibiscus and green-luscious ferns, she could have had a flower store if she desired. Once Mama established the garden, the house gradually became hers. The house appeared modest but rich with details and character. People often thought of it as a fairytale house made of crystal because of its oversized glass windows, its forest-like setting created by cedar wood logs and sheltered by guava, orange, loquat, jocote and mango trees. Guests entered the house through separate lawns of green grass bordered by lush gardens. Upon reaching the main door, they had to cross the main patio, alerting us to their presence by the sound of their footsteps on hollow wooden planks. Then, a few years later, after a few more sensual midnight negotiations between my parents, and just before the shaking of the destructive 1972 earthquake, Mama expected a new blessing: ME. "It must have been when I conceived you that you brought upon the destructive earthquake! Mama often teased me when I inquired about my birth. Later, after learning the drastic change the 1972 earthquake brought upon our country, I did not find her sense of humor very funny. According to the news the destructive earthquake destroyed about ninety percent of the city of Managua, thousands were killed, several more injured and many went without water or food for at least twenty-four hours. And to make it worse, many did not receive proper burials but were rather burnt with gasoline on the streets, as typhoid was feared. Nonetheless, happy with Mama's expectancy news, Abuela said, "*Los que Dios te quiera dar*," reinforcing her beliefs to Mama that a devout Catholic woman must bear as many children as granted by the Lord.

"Maybe this child will grow up to love the wilderness as much or more than the rest," Abuela hoped.

Her words were prophetic. Apparently, the wildlife and the rain forest did not cast the same spell on the rest of my siblings as it would on me. They seemed to favor school, where as I shared the resistance to formal education like the great poet, Rubén Darío, who after failing to stay in school, educated him himself in the town's library. After the good news of Mama's new pregnancy, and the survival of my parents' new home after the destructive earthquake, it was with open arms that they welcomed my Abuelos again. Abuela's gourmet cooking and Abuelo's tickling spoiled my brothers and sisters. My family rejoiced when the beloved Abuelos moved in once more to assist Mama into bringing a new life, even if it would be for the eighth and final time. Embracing my six-foot tall, dark and handsome Abuelo's hand, our petite, five-foot short, blond-haired, and green-eyed Abuela walked through Mama's beautiful gardens to our house, determined to be there for as long as she was needed. A rooted Roman Catholic, Abuela served as a role model. Like Abuelo, she was also a grand storyteller, and my family would listen with rapt attention as she told about the love she and Abuelo had shared.

Disowned by her family, as she had married a man of inferior status against their will, Abuela said she would love and cherish Abuelo for eternity. Holding hands day after day, they rose to the crow of the rooster and then headed to the first mass at 5:00 a.m. Dedicated to and always serving God, Abuela made sure that Mama's soul had a first class reservation in heaven. She constantly reminded Mama that it was a virtuous woman's duty to serve God and to bear children until he commanded, "No more." Disobeying such law meant a first class ticket to hell. Therefore, for many years, she jealously guarded Mama's reputation and her heavenly reservation. Three months after Amanda had left Mama, as the duty of an exemplary Roman Catholic woman would dictate, Mama became pregnant with Francisco, her second child: the wizened and studious. Later came Socorro: beautiful and determined; Ramón: the problem solver and audacious one; Juan Carlos: highly spirited and courageous; Francisca: as beautiful as Socorro, studious and golden-hearted; Benjamin: young, playful and pleasing to my parents; and, lastly, her lucky eighth—ME: the curious and rebellious one, as Mama would often describe me.

Taught with strict morals to follow, many novenas to pray, and extensive instructions on how a proper woman ought to behave, Mama served God and Papa until her womb no longer nourished life. Perhaps her fecundity was a desperate attempt to fill the emptiness Amanda had left, or simply compliance in trying to win my hopeless Papa's heart and God's divine blessing. Perhaps it stemmed from both reasons. This I do not know. Regrettably, Abuela must have forgotten to interpret the laws of God to Papa, who interpreted the law to father children with other women like a rabbit, for his own benefit. To him, adultery did not mean ungodly, and he decided that in order to secure his hard-earned land, he needed to father as many children as granted by the Lord. Destination of his holy first class ticket: Unknown. Since Mama spent most of the year in her new home in town, she occupied herself easily with seven noisy children and weekly church activities.

At home, Mama could be seen sewing by her bedroom window overlooking the cloud forests and her beloved garden, cooking on a traditional adobe stove or chasing after us with a solid leather belt. At church, Mama often preached by the altar's podium, confessed her daily sins and kneeled down before God, until she recited all prayers with modest diligence and her knees began to swell. Fearing the repossession of his land by the government, as many other landowners had faced, Papa spent most of the time in isolation at the farm. At least that was what Mama wished to believe as rumors spread of his clandestine romances. Unlike Mama, Papa would only kneel to replace a broken underground pipe, or to assist a struggling cow in delivering her calf. He could be found roaming the forest on his brown horse, replacing broken barbwire fences, spreading and drying coffee beans, cutting up sugar canes, milking the cows or routinely visiting the less fortunate, as he would call the fortune-seeking witches of the forests.

In the course of time and on a fine day in July 1973, as Mama recalled my birth, Papa sweated profusely as he waited for this unique person to come into his life. He stood in the room witnessing my birth, the same way he witnessed a calf being born. "*Apuraté, Apuraté!*" he hurried distressed Mama. "The baby has been in there for too long and needs to come meet us now." Poor Mama must have lost all of her maternity weight, perspiring and pushing, until I finally decided to face the challenges of this world.

"It's a girl!" the doctor announced. "She is bigger than a nine-pound rabbit!" He then held me upside down while slapping my butt cheeks until I released an acceptable cry. It was said that while raising her head, Mama gave me a glance of approval and then fainted.

"Was I that ugly?" I asked when Mama first told me this story.

"No!" she laughed, "But giving birth to a child of your size was not at all easy."

I could not imagine how my petite one hundred-twenty pound Mama carried me in her womb for so long. Every time I asked, she would say, "Anything is possible with God's will." Indeed, it was His will. Child number eight turned out to be a last-minute surprise for my already exhausted mother.

Ileana, 4 months old

And out of all the things that flood my memory, the place that lingers the most in my often-busy mind is the embrace of my inner paradise, beautiful and fragile, within the larger paradise of Nicaragua, which occurred in my hometown, the City of Mist. It was there where my umbilical cord detached from Mama's womb, and I became my own. Our town was a unique place to grow up. City of Mist remained constantly cooled by the misty air and plentiful rainfall. Dense clouds and a large artificial lake—a symbol of modernization barricaded it. It was a colonial town—unlike any other my eyes have seen. It witnessed my first dreams and later my nightmares. Through the awe-inspiring and at time celestial sounds of classical, folkloric and religious music, it transformed my reality into a palette of blues and violets.

Local Franciscan teachers, and at times our town priests, taught us the ways of good Catholics, along with the music of composers such as Beethoven, Bach and Mozart. They would switch the old record player, hardly visible through the long sleeves of their cassocks and instruct us to sit around in a circle, as they would play several songs. The masters' cheeks reddened at moments of inspiration as our eyes sparkled with hopes and dreams. And instead of tolling the heavy chrome church bell to announce the hour, the church would often play a classical song that resonated all over town through an oversize speaker. "Für Elise" by Beethoven was the song I remember most and it is the song that has become a bridge to my past memories. The town's people paused their activities while they listened to the concerto. Listening to the wordless melody for only a few seconds was all I needed for dreams of wonder and power to come to me. In most Latin American towns, colorful folkloric rhythms and upbeat songs serenade people. At that time, citizens from the City of Mist, however, also enjoyed different aspects of our ancestors' cultures. The moment the loud, melodic music escaped through the church's speakers, everyone paused in their chores. The bread vendors, who graciously balanced woven baskets of breads and fruits on their heads most hours of the day, rested a few seconds. The shoeshine boys at *La Plaza Central* slowed their pace; gossips took a few seconds before resuming their tales, and maids, whose main jobs were to mop the red tile floors to keep them shiny, refilled their lungs with air before they continued scrubbing. I, too, paused whatever grand activity I did at that moment and rejoiced in the divine serenity these melodic seconds would bring.

The interruption of our daily routines by the subtle melody came with a certain magic that inspired us all to dream, beyond the borders of terror and despair that were constantly threatening the country. I dreamt about life in another world, the tranquil landscapes of the forests above my home and the graceful, yet powerful silhouette of its creatures. And it was then that I often dreamt of my beloved forests to the tune of Für Elise as it blended along with the dissonance of the exotic fauna of toucans, elusive quetzals, ocelots, macaws, earth-bound and arboreal reptiles, jaguars and howler monkeys. In my dreamy mind, the forest was still perfumed by vibrant frangipanis, stubborn ferns and humid moss. Everything wild and endangered moved to the lyrical song and was lit by moonlight filtered through the dense canopy. A flock of macaws flew down to me and then opened their wings to rise swiftly. Even in the dim light, their flamboyant plumage shimmered like rainbows.

As I grew older, the best of paradise was yet to be revealed within the cloud forest. It was the perfect land for fertile coffee plantations and abundant crops, a place remote from the town, where only lightning and nature had the final say. It was there where my most exhilarating memories took place. The farm was distant and free of boundaries, the same way Mama had first seen it while holding Amanda in her arms, located in the dense wilderness of the country, a virgin paradise filled with strange wildlife. I tasted the beauty and the addiction of freedom, the type that I only felt when mounting onto my horse Lucero and galloping through the untouched landscapes without speed limits. A solemnity hardly replaceable where my ears blocked all sounds and nothing else mattered. This was also the place responsible for my stubborn resistance for school, as I never wished to leave its addictive embrace.

For years, Mama remained faithful to her children, Papa and her divine God. She did what faithful Spanish Roman Catholic women were expected to do: serve God and the husband unconditionally. She went about her daily hurdles, ignoring her husband's wrong doings and praying daily to the Lord for his generous absolution. Meanwhile, Papa's passion diverted entirely to his hard-earned land, the same land his Papa had taught him to cultivate. He rooted himself deep into the land, so out of reach that no one, neither Mama nor his first children, could extract him away. With time, his light brown hair turned silver prematurely by the constant harassment of minds ill with the thoughts of war and the actions of some Christians, who often claimed territories that did not belong to them. According to some ancestral stories shared at family dinners, we inherited the genes of our fortune-seeking, Spanish-Italian ancestors who, since the 1800's, have occupied the much sought after land of Nicaragua. They set up agricultural plantations and cattle ranches in a territory too mystical to ignore. Other relatives claimed my paternal ancestors came from Basque. To me, it no longer mattered, for some of us still ended up in the same place we stand today, landless with only the ownership of a soul tangled in the memories of a destiny.

Nicaraguans are difficult to isolate into one particular ethnicity. Some claim British ancestry and speak French and English, some speak the

Miskito indigenous language while others claim a more exotic breed, white and Amerindian ancestry, also known as Mestizos like the brown-skinned goddess who balanced a breadbasket on her head daily through the old stone road and the orphan religiously shining shoes at *El Parque Central*. Few can claim to be full-blooded of European ancestry. Two typical examples were the short, stubby, old owner of a vast rain forest land and the old, big-nosed, stubborn woman from the nearby pastry shop. At the end, they would all turn out to be known simply as *Pinoleros Nicaragüenses*, whose lives would revolve around sweet cornmeal and cacao drinks. Balbina, my big-nosed, blue-eyed paternal Abuela used to say, "Our mixing with our Mestizo ancestors turned us into great beings." And Papa, in defense of his height, would remind us, "Fine essence doesn't always come in large proportions." After listening to Abuelo's stories about our European and Amerindian ancestors, and how they founded our colonial towns across Nicaragua, I often wondered why we stayed in a country that did not embrace autonomy and equality for all.

"Just look around you," Papa would say in answer to my questions.

I looked around, just as many others had, and understood. Our ancestors founded colonial towns all across the country with the intentions of growing spices and shipping them back to their homelands. Instead of returning, they fell in love with their newly found motherland, a fertile mother whose volcanic lava flowed through the hollow craters of her distended womb. From the mountains to the oceans, she nourished the cloud forest with mist and the rain forest with tears. A stern mother, she kissed with the sun as she caressed the soil, but reprimanded her children with torrential rains and the pummeling of her thunder.

It is the discrepancy of distorted politics and enchanting landscapes, which often floods my deepest memory. I am now an adopted daughter of a new land, the United States of America, but from time to time, my birth land of Nicaragua knocks at my door and pleads for me not to forget, as if from one day to the next her natural splendor might cease to exist. Papa, whose roots remain stranded in that land, comes as well to remind me about my first home. "Once you marry the Nicaraguan soil, you are never granted a divorce," he proudly admitted one day as he inhaled the scent of the humid soil, while digging a hole with his short and stout finger on the softened ground. As he planted a new seed, I joined him on his reforestation routine for every time he cleared the land to make room for his agricultural fields, he would be conscious of the need to keep the forests as virgin as possible.

"We have plenty of trees, Papa. Why are you planting more?"

"There can never be enough," he explained patiently, while inspecting his surroundings with apparent sorrow. "I have contributed to enough damage by making room for cultivations and our cattle, but it is never too late."

Papa loved the land he stood on. No one could blame him for loving her so much. The same captivating land gave birth to the inspiration of her son Rubén Darío, the father of modernism, who spread his wings around the world, and who in 1916, returned only to rest eternally under the soil of his motherland.

Undeniably, the spell of the land made it disheartening for its war-abused citizens to abandon it. Rooted to the forests like Papa, after the repossession of their land, many risked losing their lives or worse, surrendering their daughters' virginities. They flew away from their native land of Nicaragua and became exiles in unknown territories. And during times of anguish and after becoming aliens in other countries, it was without doubt that they often came to hate themselves for loving Nicaragua so. And somehow, as provincial civilians, the trap of distorted politics entangled us and as a result, the land and the struggle to keep our family together came at a high price.

3

On How a Destiny Unfolds

Ileana, 2 years old with Francisco

L ET ME TELL you a story from the past,
because without the past the present would not

be. Perhaps, if the father of the Sandinista Front, General Augusto César Sandino, the man whose face is painted on the humid Nicaraguan walls, and whose ghost still roams around its potholed streets, had allowed my maternal grandfather, Abuelo Lalo, to die on that foggy day and Mama and Papa did not marry, my destiny might have been a different one. It is undoubtedly one of the laws of life that we learn where and when we are born, but not how, when or where we will die.

My story began before my birth. The year was 1933. At that time, Mama was not yet born. Witnessing the possible execution of his father and grounded to the moist soil sat my young uncle Germán, tremulous as a deer. It appeared one of the General's trusted men had a personal quarrel with a man who would later become my grandfather, and was determined to get him out of the way, the same way he cleared his path throughout the forest, using only a weathered machete. Unfortunately for my Abuelo—a man known for his dark skin, languid posture, above-average height and righteous demeanor—his death would not be a quick one, as expected from a bullet shot straight to the head. His assailant wanted him to suffer; he was going to sever his head or neck, maybe both, depending on the tenderness of my Abuelo's skin, or the sharpness of his weathered machete. My uncle Germán never forgot the man. Pedrón Altamirano was his name. He was a known killer presumed to eradicate anything that crossed his path, but just as

Pedrón began to secure his feet on the ground, another soldier arrived, none other than the right hand of General Sandino, José Rosa Irías.

"Leave that man to me!" he demanded.

"Why should I leave him to you? I'm going to kill him," refused Pedrón.

People often said that other than General Sandino, José Rosa Irías would be the only one who bore a rifle. Now, pointing the rifle towards Pedrón, he ordered the release of my Abuelo. "If you don't leave him to me, this will be the end of you," José Rosa added while pointing the rifle to his head.

The men were about to challenge each other when suddenly, galloping on a beautiful horse, wearing an oversize cowboy hat, high laced boots and a rifle, appeared a man known as the Men's General—Augusto César Sandino. On that day, the young General rode in the company of his beautiful wife, Blanca Aráuz, a telegrapher and a relative to my father's family. General Sandino later became a national hero known for his bravery who fought with an army of farm workers against the intervention of the United States in Nicaragua during the years of the Somoza regime. He wished for Nicaragua to enjoy the fruits of peace and democracy but was later assassinated by Somoza's national guard on his way to sign a peace treaty, ensuring his eternal residency in Nicaragua as a martyr amid the painted and humid walls of the country.

Upset by what he encountered and after spotting a sorrowful young boy clinging to a Royal Cedar tree, General Sandino himself pointed his long rifle at Pedrón and demanded the immediate release of my Abuelo. Without hesitation, Abuelo lifted his son off the humid ground, nodded his head down in appreciation towards the young General and soon after that relocated his family away from the forest. There is no doubt the General saved my Abuelo's life on that day, and for that, I am grateful. For many years the irony of this day resonated in my mind, for every time I heard this story, I knew it was meant for me to be born. It was thanks to that gloomy day, as Abuelo would say, that General Sandino ensured Mama's birth—and later mine. It was also said that the General might have had noble intentions for the country. However, after his death, the nightmares that followed were not simple bed-wetting ones, but rather the type that make you wish to have never been born.

"It was not meant for me to die on that day, but surely there are many different ways to kill a man," Abuelo would often say as he retold his story again.

I did not comprehend the true meaning behind his story then. To me, a person would either be alive and buoyant, or dead and forgotten. Abuelo enjoyed many more years in the company of his wife, Abuela Chunita, my maternal grandmother. She was a petite, fair-skinned woman, and an exemplary Roman Catholic who aimed solely for the purification of her soul in order to ensure eternal peace in heaven. Therefore, she allowed her body to conceive as many children as granted by the Lord. Sadly, her first ten pregnancies resulted in miscarriages. However, Abuela never relented; she continued to pray to the lord for more children until eventually her womb retained the last five, Mama being the last child.

4

Everlasting Summers

Ileana, riding her horse at the farm.

ONCE UPON a summer night there was moonlight and a soft serenade, mesmerizing my world, caressing my landscape. "Good memories should outweigh bad ones," the elders often said. Plus, it is easier for me to host your journey through this reading if I continue with the beginning of jovial times, the ones that kept me up on my feet and often reminded me that hope should be the last thing you should ever lose. The memories of everlasting summers at my parents' farm began in 1978 and have no ending date since they still linger in my mind—as if yesterday is still today. Once the school year ended for all of my siblings, we quickly prepared for a much-anticipated retreat to the farm. Waiting for us by the roadside, there always stood my handsome Papa, holding the horses for us to ride. His flirtatious face had an irresistible smile of thin curved lips that made Mama nearly drop to her knees. Of course, she would not admit it, but I could see how she felt for him. I, too, loved him immensely. The farm felt like a different world. The moment we began to journey through the forest, Mama and I could feel the serenity that only nature could provide.

Our lungs filled with the abundant oxygen supplied by the endless varieties of plants and trees. All of them spoiled our eyes with views of exotic paintings free of charge. We galloped on our horses and indulged in creamy, sweet mamey fruit, purchased from the last roadside fruit stand. Soon illnesses and worries would fade away. I would circle back and ride past Mama several times on my young horse Lucero, and then finally wait for her to catch up to me with her tireless old Clydesdale. There was no doubt in my mind that Mama and her horse were meant for each other. They were minimum risk takers and took advantage of every second of the hour available to them to climb to our mountain home. Waiting for them to catch up was agonizing, since for whatever reason Mama needed to take several breaks, and I could barely wait to reunite with my animal friends and wild surroundings. As we got closer, we rested on a hill near the forest that overlooked the farm and our log house. Using Papa's binoculars, we could see the log house supported by mahogany pillars, our farm dogs Ladrón and Misuterrí guarding the house and the cows grazing. We could also see Papa's maid Lucrecia feeding the pigs while her father Don Cito sat outside on a wooden stool enjoying a homemade tobacco leaf cigar, his sun-dried mouth squeezing the cigar with pleasure. We could even see the chickens pecking around the apple-red coffee plantations, the white geese near the pond and Mama's favorite orchards. We could see fruit trees overweighed by creamy avocados, juicy citruses, and a wide variety of sun-sweetened bananas. The inviting house came into sight, quiet and isolated, waiting for us to fill it with our dreams and reckless adventures.

My legs bowed and ached, tired from the long horse ride. We dashed inside the first house occupied by the farm keeper and her two sons, Santos and Chacho. Upon arrival, Lucrecia welcomed us with a shy smile. She appeared forever young. Her long black hair now reached her waist and her brown skin, except on her hands, was still plump and radiant. The only thing that revealed the passage of time were her dry and brittle hands, damaged by the daily scrubbing of clothes, the grinding of maize on a stone and the clamping of tortillas made for breakfast, lunch and dinner. Thorn cuts in her hands revealed that she had also chopped wood for the crackling fire that often hypnotized my senses. Lucrecia was content to have us back as she would rarely interact with anyone other than the animals at the farm. She served us hot red beans cooked in a clay pot with the taste of dirt, fresh cheese from the morning milking and corn tortillas she had made for dinner. After chatting with her children and exchanging adventure stories while chewing on sugar cane, we headed to our old house and helped Mama dust the bed and check for bed bugs. Papa quickly brought wood for the fire stove made out of adobe and river rocks. Mama scooped the settled ash that remained from our last visit. I was happy; I felt right at home, experiencing the jitters that the wild surroundings, including the rats that ate the corn stalks in our crop storage, added to the feeling of bliss the farm life would bring.

"¡BAM, BAM, *un ratón*!" Mama shouted while she pounded on an overweight rat with a broom.

"¡Ya!" Papa said as he grimly stepped on it with his heavy boots until the long bare and pink tail of the rat stopped moving. Watching the rat breathe its very last breath made me sick to my stomach, regardless of how natural an event this would be at the farm. If there is such a thing as a resolution, mine was to accept the way things were at the farm. I could not succeed in getting used to the killing of animals, just as I could not control the chills some of the animals would give: long-horned cows sleeping with their large eyes open, snakes slithering beneath fallen leaves and cobwebs everywhere I turned to. When at long last Mama and Papa caught up with each other, they would sit by the fire drinking warm coffee, one cup after another, until every piece of wood burned up slowly and the warm ashes fell onto the river rocks that lay below. That night I could not beckon any sleep, as the image of the rat's dying tail kept haunting my mind and the dissonance of the wild added to my anxiety. I had yearned for this moment for so long, and once there, I no longer knew what to do next. My sisters Francisca and Socorro laughed after teasing the boys with jokes and the boys spooked Benjamin and me with stories of the wild.

"It was midnight when the black bull blended within the darkness, his eyes flaming red and it smelled of sulfur…" My brother Juan Carlos retold while adding malevolent sounds to the fable.

Benjamin and I were frightened but succumbed ourselves to sleep with our heads beneath our pillows, and awoke the next day to greet the crisp morning at the farm. Our first morning went by fast as we rediscovered every inch of the landscape and revisited the wildlife. My brother and I pestered the red ants up in the hills. They were always busy carrying pieces of green leaves.

We searched for snakes with our long sticks and prepared empty jars for firefly hunts at night. Then, after observing the daily herding and the milking of over one hundred cattle, I would follow my loving and at times deceitful brother Benjamin, who was followed by Santos and Chacho, to the bull's corral. This was the place where the chicken laid warm eggs in nests assembled in the surrounding bushes of the corral. It was also the place of rest for Papa's favorite red Brahman bull. His big hump and loose skin hung under his neck. The corral was fenced with partial barbwire and wooden post fences, heavily saturated with cow manure and scattered rocks to prevent erosion. I don't know what transpired through my mind that particular morning at the beginning of our stay, but I decided to get in trouble and fall for my brother's taunting. The boys decided to tease me into a challenge with the bull, while they stared at me with their brown and mischievous eyes. "We bet you're like a chicken and won't cross the corral, pick an egg from the chickens' nest and run back to us before the bull chases you," they challenged.

"I'm NOT challenged! It'll take a while for that ton of meat to get to me!" I assured them, more concerned about their persistent goading. "Just watch me!"

"You don't have to do it anymore!" Benjamin retracted.

"Now you fret over me? I'll show you who the chicken here really is!" I taunted.

I bent to go under the barbed wire fence as the boys held it in disbelief. I then headed slowly into the corral. My water boots quickly sank into the soiled ground as the smell of the rancid, processed pasture, now turned into manure, assaulted my nostrils. Far back, the bull stood still, so I figured that I could cross quickly, steal an egg from a hen and be back before the menacing bull noticed me. I set off walking very slowly in the stone corral and tried hard not to upset the bull's peace. Well, I made it all the way across and even had time to choose from the chickens' nests. I managed to retrieve one warm egg from a chicken but not without a fight as she became angry with me and started clacking. It might have been that alerting clack the chicken made that nearly turned my day into a tragedy.

"Get back!" the boys shouted.

Benjamin jumped up and down, holding his head and looking frightful towards the bull. I looked back to assure that the bull was still standing far away but quickly noticed that he was no longer at his spot. The animal charged at me furiously as his hump and loose skin moved from side to side.

"Help!" I called out while running back towards my brother as I desperately attempted to out-run the infuriated bull.

Thankfully, I escaped and headed back to the boys where they were yelling for me to run even faster. I could barely feel the ground as I outstripped the wind beneath my feet. The egg had left my hand, and I could feel my body diminishing to the size of a working ant as the bull approached closer and closer. At one point, I cursed the idea of going to the corral altogether and wished I had stayed inside the house under the safety of Mama's apron. Barely beating the red bull by what seemed to be a few centimeters, I made it to the fence where my brother held up the barbed wire again, this time with a somber and pale face.

"Hurry, *chigüina!*" he begged at the top of his lungs, pulling the rest of my body to the other side of the fence. Then latching onto my brother I stared at the red bull prancing by.

"You are okay now, you featherbrained girl!" my brother scolded. I could feel my legs wiggle uncontrollably.

"I don't know what made that bull so angry! His mouth was full of white foam!" I said.

"Bulls don't like little kids, particularly girls!" Chacho added, laughing and exposing a few rotten teeth.

"Now you tell me!" I reproached running home to Mama.

"This never happened, or we won't let you play with us again!" Santos then threatened.

I kept our bull adventure a secret, as I knew that if I had said something, we might get leather marks on our backs, and since it was in my nature to refute punishment with all my skill, I would have gotten even more strikes on my body. I decided not to mention it, as I could still feel the sting of my last beating for disobedience. By dawn the sky near the horizon transformed into a palette of red, orange and yellow hues, announcing the retreat of the sun as it descended slowly and the sky became a curtain of either dense fog or mesmerizing starry, summer nights. As a child it appeared to me that the most unforgettable moments in the wilderness took place at the retreat of the sun. The summer nights were short and illuminated by the most captivating and imaginably glowing full moon. The paths were as visible at night as in daylight. Every critter in the forest, from the owls to the sloth, seemed to celebrate those resplendent starry summer nights.

> *Saltate una rana,*
> *saltate dos,*
> *talves podras contar*
> *mas de dos.*

Skip a frog skip by two; maybe you could count past two, I chanted, nearly stepping on flirty-flecked frogs as they joined the cacophony of the wildlife. What's more, I went around capturing as many

66

fireflies as I could with my empty plastic jar, only to awake the next morning to see their lights had forever turned off.

A large hill loomed over our house. I would climb to the top and rest before rolling down. The hill lay just under higher hills that held the cloud forest, and I often wondered how far away the moon really was. Staring directly at its dazzling light, at times I could see the shape of a rabbit sitting on it; at other times the same creature appeared to be a wolf. I would lie back on the grass, drifting away to a world full of wonders as suddenly giggling sounds brought me back to reality, and I soon realized that the moon had different effects on others.

"Stop your madness," Francisca demanded as Julio, an admirer from a local farm, played a serenade with his nylon string guitar.

Illuminated by moon glow, my beautiful sister sat on the grassy hill. The light bathed her round face, soft skin, long dark hair and big brown-greenish eyes. I thought her admirer might drool as he played his guitar and sang to her, giving her the typical conquistador stare of a Spanish lover whose heart might come to a halt, if his conquest did not fulfill. The concentrated and intoxicating scent of his 7-Machos cologne penetrated my nostrils as the wind carried it my way. I could tell he spent a few minutes preparing for his conquest—his hair combed back and slicked with hair pomade. Although Francisca enjoyed the courting, she spent most of her time dreaming about her future and creating homemade skin treatments to ensure her endless beauty: rose water to relax the skin, cold water to make the hair more lustrous and avocado, and salt and olive oil to moisturize and exfoliate her already supple skin. Her future goals might have involved being most lovely of all women and perhaps attending college or becoming an influential businesswoman.

"¡Ya es hora de dormir muchachos!" Mama called, interrupting our summer dreams.

It was time for all visitors to leave and for us to go to sleep. We all went inside the house, whining and panting. Mama greeted us with the warm aroma of Marquezote bread, and fresh milk, ensuring celestial dreams as always. Built as one of nature's gifts, Papa's farm log house reigned amid the forest. The bedrooms were small but cozy. The kitchen was plainly equipped with a long piece of the sought-after Granadillo wood that was used as a basin to wash dishes and to grind crops, and a stone wood-fired stove. Papa built the farmhouse with his bare hands using only sturdy logs culled from the verdant forests, home to trees, pastures and creatures whose hair and skin were lit by stunning sunsets, moonlight and fireflies. The modest log house was the only civilized thing in sight. Like our house in the City of Mist, this, too, appealed to all the senses with its variety of aromatic flowers, scenic landscapes, and its vegetable and herb gardens. However, the flowers at the farmhouse were wild, and domesticated only by Mama's green thumb, as she never failed to make anything appear its best. At times, it seemed to me that the dogs had been groomed, the horse's teeth cleaned, and the pigs knew better than to smile with their filthy mouths. At my young age, all I could do was daydream about growing up quickly so that I, too, could hear serenades and receive gifts like my two older sisters. Maybe someday, I thought, I too might be serenaded.

These were the times of dreams, hopes and innocent amusements. These are the episodes of our life that come to visit me every now and then, through the foliage of my reminiscences and Mama's retelling. There was so much to do, enjoy and discover. Some of my favorite things to do at the farm were horseback riding and blackmailing my sisters and their boyfriends, in exchange for juicy chewing gum and the privilege of listening to their adult conversations. One evening, Mama scolded me to go away, *"¡Veté a jugar!"* She demanded, annoyed by my mere presence. Unwilling, I remained in the kitchen corner listening to what would be an endless argument between my parents. I did not go away as instructed, but instead dragged my doll Muñcca by the hair and pretended to play with her. "What fun is it to play with a useless doll, if I could listen to you instead?" I grumbled.

"Your time will come," Mama assured, overlooking the corner as if she had always known I was there. "Do not rush life, Ileana; just remember that not even the leaves from the trees move without God's will."

Upset, I retreated to bed ignorant of what she meant and anxious for the crow of the rooster to announce the beginning of a new day so that I could chase after Papa in the morning. Always ready, and the first one up! I knew Papa's routine inside out: pants were first, wallet, knife and water boots next, followed lastly by his shirt and denim jacket. Every night before he went to bed, he left his clothes in the order in which he would wear them the next day.

"You must always be ready to dress and run. You never know when lightning might strike," he had said once.

Confused, I asked, "Lightning? What difference would it make if it struck us with our clothes on?"

Reacting to me with his playful grin, he responded, "I hope you never find out." Finally, my ongoing inquiries tested his patience and he commanded me to help Mama in the kitchen. My brothers should have taken my place there, but the challenges of early rise were too much for them to handle.

"¡*Despierten, hombres*!" Papa scolded, "¡*Despierten*!"

It took a wrathful army to wake them up. They preferred to tame books in lieu of horses and dress in polyester pants instead of Levi jeans. Their dreams were not to manage Papa's humble farm, but rather to tame nunchucks and go on incredible Hollywood action adventures as seen on television.

70

Posters of Bruce Lee and Chuck Norris displayed in their rooms, boldly revealed their democratic and dreamy characters.

"What have I done to deserve this? How could it be that out of many *chigüines*, I don't have one to follow after me?" Papa often lamented.

"I'm here, Papa," I offered.

Papa walked away with me by his side, without uttering a word. Then with a smile he pulled me up to his shoulders, carrying me to our horses as we saddled up to what would be another splendid summer day. I am not sure what made the farm my most beloved paradise. Perhaps it was the mysteries of the forest, the shy exotic animals that were so hard to see that when I spotted one, it felt miraculous, or perhaps it was just the sound of howler monkeys that would break the simplicity of life. It was a place to escape from the rush of daily life, and the conspiracies of society. The rumors of an abusive dynasty, and the anger of the leftist rebellion, did not seem to contaminate the beauty and tranquility of the solemn landscape. Boundaries were nowhere in sight; the horizon appeared to have no beginning or end. The forest-barricaded farm was the ideal place, where a free-spirited child like me could easily roam around all day and not be missed. Upon returning with Papa from sensational adventures, I would wander happily through the plantation fields and orchards. One day I entangled myself in their delectable wonders. Electricity did not reach the farm, and as a result we had no refrigeration. Therefore, the farmhouse was a self-sustained place where everything came directly from the land. The many fields offered organic, sun-ripened bananas of many varieties—my favorite and the sweetest baby bananas, robust coffee, and sweet sugar cane. The orchards also provided fruits and vegetables such as oranges, limes, guava, guanabana, mamey, squash, beans, and corn.

During my daily explorations, I would eat sun-ripened bananas that were within my reach, and sucked on sun-sweetened red coffee beans. When done, I would head back home; but one day, stepping recklessly over sticks and leaves, I became aware of a swift movement under the carpet of dry leaves, just a few inches away from my feet. At that moment the cautiousness my parents had attempted to instill in me should have taken root, but rather, the itching curiosity of the unknown prompted me to pick up a long stick and uncover the mysterious creature that lay hidden. A dazzling brightly-colored coat was revealed with hypnotizing black and red rings, as a captivating snake slithered angrily along the ground.

What a charmer, I thought, unable to cease from teasing it. The swift snake threatened towards me as I invaded her territory. I quickly and instinctively hopped over it with my high-water boots and decided to run away.

"¡Papa!" I cried out, approaching Papa who was working close to home. "You won't believe if I describe to you the pretty snake I discovered under the fallen leaves!"

"What kind?"

"A bright red and black ringed snake, Papa."

Papa became upset. "Never tease a venomous snake again. That sounds like a king coral snake! If it had bitten you, you would not be telling the story," he nervously explained. Apparently, it was not yet my time to leave my precious world. Agitated by a rapid heartbeat resulting from sucking on sweet red-ripened coffee beans, I immediately decided to persuade Papa again to take me on yet another exciting experience for the afternoon.

"Let's ride Papa!" I suggested, ignoring his recent rhetoric. Desiring to gallop with my brown horse Lucero, I begged Papa to get him ready for me.

"Go ahead," he finally gave in, "just be careful not to jump over any fallen trees left by the storm."

I assured him that I wouldn't do it. Promising only to walk the horse, I headed towards a recently flattened area plowed by Papa's oxen with a wooden plow, but freedom in my innocent mind involved riding that brown horse and exploring the forest itself arrayed endlessly with the wild grasses and flowers. The embrace of the virgin forest and its free-flowing springs alone would satisfy me; its call became too enticing. I cannot recall exactly how much I weighed then, but I was growing up to be a very thin child, despite my very high infancy weight. I must have weighed only about seventy pounds. I think the horse forgot I was riding him. Lucero began to gallop rapidly, making it hard for me to open my eyes. The breeze echoed past my ears; my heartbeat increased with restless excitement and nothing mattered beside the joy I felt at that point. Relying solely on instinct, I let the horse take me away, held my head up, tightened my hands on the reins, kept my legs on the saddle, and let him go wild and untamed—the way God meant for him to be. The rapture of the moment overcame any proper judgment until my frantic Papa's voice interrupted my revelry.

"Stop that horse," he demanded.

I turned my head and there he was, urgently chasing after me. But before I could react, he came to grip my horse, just before he jumped over a deep trench, where a pond was fed by a spring bubbling from the ground. Unsure of what had just happened, my attention suddenly diverted to the pond. On its surface water lilies grew; calla flowers and a few orchids hid in the shadows. I became thirsty by the fresh and sparkling water that flowed out of the spring. And once again, Papa abruptly interrupted my reverie.

"I'm tired. You will no longer ride a horse!"

I felt disheartened to have caused him such worry, but the moments I spent racing on Lucero brought me feelings not many people encounter in a lifetime. The instant addiction to freedom, wonderfully heart-pounding freedom, so scarce in life, made my heart skip a beat and forever changed my way of being. How subtle, how sweet, yet how frail freedom can be! I had felt as if the world belonged to me, without boundaries or rules to follow. For that short moment, it was just my horse, the wind, and I. It was then, that dreaming about my wild ride, I welcomed another night, more moonlight, and another serenade.

Luna que se quiebra	Broken moon
sobre las tinieblas	over the clouds
de mi soledad	of my loneliness.
Que vuelva ya	Return now.
Dile que la quiero	Tell her that I love her,
dile que la estraño...	tell her that I miss her...

This song serenaded many nights as young men attempted desperately to conquer my sisters' hearts. Once the word spread that we had arrived at the farm, the evenings became almost as busy as the days. Young men asked to speak with my sisters, hoping to declare a romantic victory. My brothers decided whom they would allow, through arm wrestling and gambling competitions, since it was the best tactic they could conjure to filter out the weaklings. As part of the match, each proud man demonstrated his prowess with the guitar in what became a long night full of romantic songs and hand-to-hand combat. Juan Carlos displayed his overworked nunchuck muscles as he defeated his friend Julio in a hand-to-hand match, his dimples deepening with satisfaction. Francisco showcased his nylon string guitar abilities as he sang along with his friend Bronco, his skinny fingers caressing the chords with considerable precision. At a table lighted by a lantern, Ramón focused deeply on the next set of cards for the five-córdoba bills that summoned his name. My sisters Francisca and Socorro watched and cheered for whoever won the daring matches. Benjamin hung onto Bronco's shoulders, and after begging for chewing gum, I retreated to the kitchen to inquire about Mama's dinner fixes.

Back in the kitchen, oblivious to what went on in the main room, Mama constructed and tasted her favorite boiled beans and recently killed armadillo stew, assuring every bite's exquisite perfection. The unfortunate armadillo came to the farm to steal chickens and instead ended up on our platters. Such was the usual fate for animals that crossed our farm: deer for dinner, skunk for lunch and bird soup for the feverish chill that comes with the common cold. If it was an edible animal that wandered into our farm on a hungry day, it qualified for a first class ticket to our dinner table. Mama added a pinch or two of fresh peppermint and sage and prepared her gourmet dish slowly and vigilantly. Observing with nervous sentiment and a sudden loss of appetite, I followed Mama to the dining table. I wished for other armadillos to become smarter and not allow the might of Papa to catch them off guard. Wearing a flowery apron, and pulling her hair back into a ponytail, Mama served dinner to everyone. She signaled to Papa to come to the table, but he ignored her call as he continued to sit on his favorite wooden rocker, re-reading his old almanac. Mama then tapped him on his shoulder with stern determination and prompted him once more to join us at the table. Setting his almanac upside down on the chair, he walked up to the table with his typical fatigued look, sat on the main chair overlooking everyone and directly facing Mama as she sat across from him. A large, yet subtle distance between them became evident as everyone ate and spoke in hushed tones. Sitting along the side of the table were my sisters who flirted discreetly with their friends, and my brothers who mischievously challenged the boys to a later match. My brother Benjamin, the youngest of the boys, sat next to Papa and I next to Mama, wondering what went on between my parents. That night everyone gave the impression to have had a fabulous time, except my parents. After hours of fun games, singing, sucking on sugarcane sticks, and saying goodbye to my sisters' suitors, we went to sleep. My parents did not. Unable to sleep by my parents' hushed talk, I sneaked through the hallway to listen to their conversation. My knees trembled as I crossed the dark hallway filled with corn stalks and overly nourished rats, but my curiosity ruled beyond all matters.

"*Sinvergüenza*, leave me alone," Mama demanded as Papa tried to wrap his hairy arms around her thinning waist.

"What is wrong with you, have you gone mad?" he asked.

"Were you able to fix the broken fence again?"

"A man has to do what he must."

"Have someone who doesn't know you well enough buy you for a peso, you old fox," she reproached pushing him away and pointing to a bruised mark on his neck.

"¡Loca!" he called her while walking away.

"Next time, make sure you drown in the river before you set foot in this house this way!" Mama added.

She always seemed to have the last say. Mama then began to weep quietly into what she thought was her sole despair. She sat on a chair pressing on her stomach, and for the first time, I saw Mama in serious pain. Her skin appeared translucent, her waistline thinner and her hair less lustrous. I hid behind the cornstalks in the hallway confused and troubled about Mama who suffered a lot. The image I had witnessed followed me for a while, until I finally had the courage to go to Mama's arm and offer comfort.

"Come *mi niña*," Mama called, kissing my forehead.

"Mama, I could stay and pray with you if you like," I offered.

"Here, hold each bead of the rosary with your thumb and index finger as you move to the next bead while we pray," Mama instructed, as she held onto a golden crucifix, made the sign of the cross and recited the Apostle's Creed.

Mama then continued to recite Our Father, while holding onto the large bead of the rosary. My job was simply to recite a Hail Mary for faith, charity and hope by holding onto each of the three small beads, then reciting the Glory Be to the Father after the third Hail Mary, recalling the first Rosary Mystery and reciting again Our Father on the next large bead. But by the time we reached the tenth Hail Mary, I began to lose track of the beads as Mama continued to recite a Glory Be to the Father and the Fatima prayer while she reflected on the mystery. Hope began to fill my heart when we approached the fifth mystery as the rosary customarily concludes. Not Mama. She continued with another Hail Mary, Holy Queen, intentions to the Holy Father—and a final Hail Mary until my eyes began to wander to the glow of her rosary by the light of the fire, that reflected on every bead, a rainbow of celestial colors. After a while, my fingers kept slipping away from the pearly beads, and the rosary became penitence as I could barely keep my eyes from closing and my sleepiness began to weigh over me as every time I opened my eyes to continue praying, my heart nearly exited my chest. I eventually lost track of the beads, but continued to hold onto them diligently as Mama threatened to start all over and would begin to sing a song she knew would surely keep me awake.

"El demonio al oido te está diciendo, deja misas y rosarios, seguí durmiendo…" Mama sang with a teasing tone.

The song stated that the devil instructed in my ear to leave masses and rosaries and to continue sleeping. Therefore, I persisted to slide the beads between my index finger and my thumb, until finally the devil succeeded at putting me to sleep. Lastly, Mama and Papa, too, went to bed, each with their backs turned away from each other. Papa's loud snores joined the cacophony of the frogs. Much later, I awoke to the sounds of love serenades my sisters' spells had brought. Under the persuasion of the moonlight and the symphony of wildlife, the courting went on as the young men, who had gone home but had returned, played their guitars and sang romantic melodies outside my sisters' bedrooms. While my parents slept, I quietly went to see the commotion. Always the first one up when she heard the young men singing late at night, Francisca brushed her long, black hair and showed her beautiful face through the window. Socorro, on the other hand, loved to sleep, and as if she felt she needed her beauty rest, she would keep on sleeping. Otherwise, she, too, would get up from bed, and glance quickly at the mirror, removing her hair barrette and allowing her wavy hair to rest onto her thin waistline. Yawning, and a bit annoyed, she opened the window and placed her hands to her face as she listened with apparent disinterest. She knew the aspiring princes would not go away until she acknowledged their presence. I couldn't wait to grow up. I kept drinking milk and rinsing my hair with chamomile water so that I might also be as desired as my sisters. That way, when someone would serenade me, I would go to sleep, ready to awaken by those love songs. In the meantime, I only practiced by looking out my window like them.

"Come to bed," Mama interrupted. She found me looking out my window, with a look of pretended love-struck feeling on my face. "There's no rush to deal with those," she added.

She led me to my bed, kissed and drew the sign of the cross onto my forehead with her right thumb for what would have been the third time that night. I dreamt of endless moonlight and serenades, all of them for me. My suitors would bring different melodies each night, and the moon only became more alluring and brighter with time. The following morning, usual routines continued. But that morning, Mama rose earlier than usual. She carried an old woven basket on her waist, and appeared thinner than the day before as she placed it by her side and began to scrub her clothes on a stone, using homemade pork soap and water from the fountain. My eyes filled with fear, as the water appeared to turn red from the rags Mama scrubbed so diligently. Mama looked ill, and the rags were never-ending. I did not know why they were that color but knew that Mama's pale skin had something to do with it. After scrubbing the rags with hurried desperation,

Mama began to hang them on a clothesline Papa set up for her. I ran to her as her body softened and Mama fell to the ground.

"Mama, what's wrong?" I asked with tears rolling down my eyes as I called for help.

Papa was up and running at the first crow of the rooster, along with every worker at the farm. Lucrecia was getting ready to grind the coffee and the maize for tortillas but rushed outside to my call. My sisters and brothers slept until awakened by all the commotion.

"Your Mama needs to rest and eat more red bean soup to replenish the lost blood," explained Lucrecia. Convinced that red bean soup is all Mama needed, I headed back outside, still confused, and continued to hang the remaining rags for Mama. Later in life, Mama underwent a hysterectomy and I would be her last child.

I was always up before my siblings, wearing either my water boots if it was wet or my old leather shoes and blue jeans. I preferred no shoes but Mama wouldn't allow it. I would hang over the fence witnessing the morning herding of cows. On that day, however, as our vacation was coming to an end, my sisters woke much earlier than usual.

"Today is the farewell party!" they exclaimed, "Get up everyone! We have much to do." Rushing with their towels to the pools of the nearby springs, they bathed and took a long time playing and swimming. I also bathed but not for long as I was convinced my "natural" body was clean enough and did not need much scrubbing.

"¡Ven aca cochina!" Francisca taunted as she pulled and scrubbed me fervently with a ball of moss and scented pork soap, while cursing my filth.

There was one pool, the mysterious and forbidden one that had a carpet of fallen leaves. It was said by the locals that if you stepped on those leaves, the pool would swallow you alive. Upset, my skin irritated from Francisca's rough treatment, I dipped my feet into it as my brothers joined my sisters and teased to throw each of them into the other pools.

"Ay!" Socorro cried, and everyone ran to her aid. She had slipped into the perilous pool, almost knocking me over but barely held onto the rim of the pool.

"I got her!" Juan Carlos quickly grabbed her arm and pulled her out of the pool. Later, Socorro swore that she felt a strong pull when she fell into the water. We took her word for it.

Shaken, and no longer fooling around, we retreated back home, more conscious and respectful of danger behind the allure of the forest. The preparation for the party continued and my brother Benjamin and I could barely wait for it to begin. We knew that it would bring an assortment of treats we were not allowed to enjoy, for after the kind advice of our family dentist, Mama had put us both on a strict diet. Our taste buds did not get to savor anything scrumptious. Moreover, she truly expected us to follow such unreasonable advice with open arms. Unjust is the price an innocent child has to pay when evil cavities attack the teeth. Determined to enjoy some of the best things life had to offer, I wisely decided to lead my brother into a sweet expedition, despite Mama's rules.

"Don't worry!" I assured Benjamin, "This party is for us as well, and I have a plan to make sure we are a part of it."

Feeling astute, I thought that ordinary adult routines were undoubtedly children's best friends. As always, food needed tables to hold it, and tables needed long tablecloths to decorate them. Once the party began, we hid under the tables to steal the forbidden foods. Sweet indulgence went on for what felt like hours, until we were obliged to surrender due to my brother's painful cry from an unbearable stomachache. The tablecloth was lifted, and we were faced with the loveliest, most gentle, and yet the scariest face you can ever come across— Mama's. Pulling us out from under the table by our ears, Mama sent us straight to bed. While Mama was busy escorting us to our bedroom, my sisters continued to dance with their suitors and Francisca allowed Branicio to steal a kiss from her as we left the room. Forcing a spoonful of Milk of Magnesia down both of our throats in an attempt to rid us of our sweet indulgences, Mama bawled us out about our bright idea. Chastised or not, I must confess I enjoyed every bite! I had to wait patiently for my time to come. Who knew what surprises would be in store for me? Again, I dreamt that night hoping that someday I too would become a happily blessed and courted young woman like my sisters. This would be too far in the future to predict, but one much anticipated by me.

Cock a doodle doo! Cock a doodle doo! The cock crowed; it was 5:00 a.m.

"Ya es hora," Mama announced. She caressed my face with her warm fingers, signaling that the time had come. Everything was ready; it would soon be time to leave the farm but not before one more adventure.

I ran outside to say goodbye to my black dog Ladrón, my childhood best friend. His lustrous coat glowed, and his tongue flicked in and out of his mouth as his wagging tail begged me to play. Not needing further persuasion, I ran as fast as I could up on the hill and then rolled down it until Ladrón landed on my body and licked my face. I loved my dog, for he knew how to protect the farm and his loved ones from uninvited guests and wild predators.

"Be careful with the devil's dog!" people would warn others. "His teeth are sharp like blades; the true picture of the devil ready to prey on the weak."

They were irrational people and did not value his beauty and faithful courage because they were not friends of Ladrón. I knew better. I have learned that the devil most often disguised itself as a man.

"Come quickly!" Juan Carlos ordered me, pulling me up onto his horse.

"Where are we going?" I asked.

"I need you to pick some flowers for me."

And happy to be of service, I followed. "Don't be long," Mama urged as we quickly galloped away. We rode on the same horse. I rode on the back of the horse while Juan Carlos guided the horse's rein through the labyrinth of the forest. Upon entering the forest, we encountered an intimidating stillness. And as I wrapped my arms tightly around my brother's waist, I could feel the chilling cold sensation of his handgun fastened securely on his leather belt. It was not the first time that I had touched a gun. Father had taught us all how to use one ever since the rumors of the persisting war began. However, for some inexplicable reason, the coldness of the weapon never failed to give me chills. In the forest, the presence of humans was apparent, through the chopped logs left on the ground. We rode, followed by our most faithful friend Ladrón, to an isolated place where Juan Carlos had seen some rare orchids.

"Why do you want these particular orchids?" I asked while ardently searching.

"I wish to surprise a friend," he said, and then pointed to the top of a tree. "Look, up there!" He pulled on the reins and the horse came to a halt. We stared at a bird with sapphire and emerald feathers, and a comet's tail glimmering beneath its body.

"It's a male quetzal," he whispered. "It means good luck."

At that point, I wished to own one of those feathers more than anything I had ever desired. The iridescent blues and greens made this bird majestic, and its long tail feathers quite suitable for the raiment of emperors.

If I had just one! I thought as I imagined in my head how I was going to describe the magnificent bird to Mama. But she had already encountered its magic, a long time ago. Alas, the bird didn't drop a feather to me. My brother made a soft sound and the horse started to toddle again. As the path darkened beneath the canopy, water drops splashed down onto the leaves. I felt timid and exposed, and my imagination ran wild.

"What if we come across a jaguar or a yellow beard snake? Or worse, we could run into *La Següa,* the crying witch from the forest?" I asked using the words and phrases that had kept me spellbound when their stories had been told to me.

"Hush! Over there," Juan Carlos pointed tensely straight ahead. "Do you see those orchids?" he asked, guiding his right index finger to an especially dark patch of shade.

"Go get some, but be careful!"

I had gained a reputation among my siblings of being fearless. I didn't hesitate. I slipped off the horse to fetch the flowers. When I reached them, I stared with the same wonder that I had with the quetzal. Though the light was dim, I felt blinded by their array of color.

87

"Wow! These are amazing. Mama will love all these in her garden."

"Just grab some, and we'll leave!" Juan Carlos urged me nervous for reasons I couldn't guess at.

Enchanted, I began to grab as many as I could hold, but I didn't hold onto them for very long. Ladrón's bark startled me and the deafening sound of my brother's weapon forced me to drop the flowers. But I stood stock still as Ladrón barked with a strength I had never heard before and then ran into the forest, ignoring our cries for him to return.

"¡Ladrón, regresa!" My brother called and whistled to him.

A roar intertwined with Ladrón's alarming bark. Frightened, I ran to meet my brother halfway as he desperately pulled me up onto the horse, shot a few times up in the air and then kicked his heals into its side. We took off in haste.

"Go back! Please, go back!" I begged. Ladrón's cries ripped through the forest. My heart ached. "What's happening to him?"

"It might be a jaguar!" Juan Carlos whispered in my ear.

"What about Ladrón?"

"Hush!" he said as we left the forest. Then he warned me, "Don't even think of telling Papa!" What was he thinking? Did he really think Ladrón's absence would go unnoticed?

At the first sight of Papa, I tumbled from the horse and told him everything. "Papa, something happened to Ladrón!" I cried. Papa abruptly yanked my brother off the horse as a reminder not to wander off into the forest, especially if he was taking me along. I felt sick at not being able to save Ladrón, but before I went kaput, Papa took off with my brothers on their horses to search for him. After a while, Papa returned with empty hands and bad news on his face. Apparently, Ladrón had sacrificed his life to save mine, as one would expect from a girl's best friend.

"It was his time, and he would have done it again for you," Papa consoled me. "You must remember that this land holds wonders, including dreadful ones we must respect."

I dropped myself on the ground and began to cry. I had lost my best friend. Papa lifted me and carried me back home where Mama waited with concern. I cried until I ran out of tears. It was my first loss. I felt that life was over, and nothing could make it worse or better. However, Mama's sweet caresses and her loving understanding eventually made me realize that as long as I had love, I would be fine. Plus, I had promised to myself not to become attached to any other animal again. Eventually, we rode home to town, with long faces, longer than those of the horses that carried us. School was to begin the next day. We had to ride for about four hours, maybe more, depending on how many breaks Mama needed to take, before we reached an old precarious dirt road, and then the nearest town. It was the way Papa wanted it to be. He wished for the farm to remain inaccessible and untouched, and the forests as virgin as when he discovered it, an ambitious dream in a tantalizing land.

"Whoever wants a piece of it has to work for it," he often said.

We were becoming bowlegged children by the time we came upon the river. The foaming and crashing river was the last obstacle before reaching the dirt road that would take us back to City of Mist. Upon arriving at the river, my hands became numb from fear. Crossing the river was a living nightmare for me, as the strong waters nearly carried away our horses. A waterfall was not far from where we had to cross, and I cried as Papa pulled Lucero, my little horse, into the crushing waters of the river. Perhaps it was because of fear, but every time I crossed the river, bad luck came upon me. Papa urged the others to go ahead and wait for us on the other side. Then riding beside me, he proceeded to cross while holding Lucero's reins.

"Do you prefer to cross on the log?" Papa asked, pointing to a long log lifted up above the river to be used as a bridge for those who were crossing by foot.

"NO!" I wailed, remembering that the log would move from side to side, looser than the chords the circus clowns use to balance themselves. If I were to cross on the log, I had to balance my feet while holding onto a rope above my head, above the meandering waters awaiting my fall. Instead, I found myself with my face almost in the water. I don't know how it happened, but my saddle suddenly slid underneath the horse's belly. I faced the most horrifying current of water I'd ever seen in all of my long-lived years. Crying and screaming, I held onto my saddle. Papa quickly came to my rescue. Apparently, my saddle challenged me to face one of my worst fears and came loose. It was an unsuccessful strategy on its part, as I became even more frightful of the water's trickery. My trembling knees nearly hit each other as I slowly set foot on dry ground, while Papa adjusted the saddle.

"It must have been the water" he assured me. "It won't happen again, precious."

Looking back at the river, I saw native women by the riverbank, scrubbing their clothes on large rocks that protruded from the river. They stared at us while dipping their clothes several times in the shallow water. Watching them work and converse with each other gave me a sense of tranquility. I then wished I had been as brave as they were. The indigenous women appeared simple but strong—so vibrant, like warriors who controlled the river with the synchronized movements of their sun-kissed bodies and long black hair. I waved goodbye to them as they stared at us while we proceeded on our journey; I could almost see their calloused hands from all the scrubbing. Soon after, we drifted into our own deep thoughts as the horses' hooves pounded below us.

My brothers and sisters must have dreamed about their lives in the city about what it would be like when they returned to town. Mama possibly wondered about Papa returning to his farm alone and leaving her to spend many lonely days in the city raising seven children nearly on her own. Papa might have thought about how long it was going to take him to get back to the farm since he had the usual workload awaiting him. Benjamin definitely daydreamed about playing with the children in the neighborhood; he practiced the art of throwing *Trompos* successfully as he would often throw a wooden top on the ground. At that moment, winning games with these tops would be his only goal. I dreamt about my animal friends, the forest and the good times we had. I wished for nothing else in life than to spend time with them in the open air. I dreamt about how I would tease the red ants up the hill the next time. Would I use a thin or thick stick? I wondered if I would see the anteater again, and recalled my wild ride on my horse, the luck that followed me to the river and the sad loss of my beloved dog. I reminisced about how wonderful it felt to ride at the speed where the wind whispered into my ears to go faster. I dreamt about rolling down the green hills while the smell of wild grass gently tickled my nose. I recalled the adrenaline rush as I climbed on the swing Papa made up on a tall tree at the edge of a short cliff. Pushing forward off, I'd let my hands go, stretching them into the air as I led my body go off the swing in mid flight to land at the bottom of the hill. Feeling the cool air released by the surrounding forest, so majestic and untouched, made this experience an addictive one. Every now and then, if I concentrated enough, I could hear the sounds of monkeys and wildcats claiming their rights to the land of my dreams. Up and up I went until my stomach asked to quit.

Up and down, I went until I finally came down to the reality of the end of summer break. Many times I was convinced that I must have been born in the middle of the forest, cared for by the strange and marvelous animals that protected it; Mama only refused to admit the truth. At that moment, my brother Benjamin and I could not complain. Our childhoods were the way they were meant to be, enchanted by daily adventures and dreams those adults did not seem to acknowledge. Arriving at the city was a celebration for all, but not to us. We evaded civilization, the racket of the city, and school, too, not to mention the drastic change in role-play we quickly needed to adapt to. At school, we were no longer allowed to dirty our strictly-pressed uniforms. I no longer rose to put on my water boots and blue faded jeans. Instead, I wore knee-high white stockings, lustrous black leather shoes, pleated skirts and matching headbands. My behavior switched to the appropriate mode: sit up straight, cross my legs, speak properly and no tree climbing! My dreams reshaped to match those of my city friends.

At times, I amazed myself on how good I had become at this code switching. Evading trouble with Mama sometimes turned me into two different individuals, creating an emotional war between a civilized child and an untamed daughter of paradise.

Mama's Vigorón

Ingredients:

2 lbs. Pork Rinds	1 cabbage
2 lbs. Yucca/Cassava	4-6 carrots
1 lb. Tomatoes	Salt to taste
1-2 cloves of garlic	Banana Leaves
10+ limes to taste	

Directions:

1. Purchase store bought pork rinds or make your own by cooking pieces of pork rinds in a large pan. Do not add oil: it will release its own grease slowly. When crispy, place on another pan without oil.
2. Peel and cut the Yucca/Cassava into approximately 2-3 inch pieces, add garlic and salt, and boil until soft.
3. Shred cabbage into small strips; place in a large bowl.
4. Chop ripe tomatoes into small-medium squares and mix with the cabbage.
5. Peel and grate carrots. Then add to the cabbage mix.
6. Cut limes and squeeze all of the juice. Then pour into the salad and mix well.
7. Add salt to taste.
8. Allow for cabbage, tomatoes and carrots to soak in the limejuice for a few minutes before serving.
9. Use banana leaves instead of plate or for decoration.
10. Place pork rind at the bottom of the plate/banana leaves.
11. Add cabbage, tomatoes, and carrots on top of pork rinds.
12. Add pieces of boiled Yucca/Cassava.
13. Add salt or limes to taste. Enjoy with or without utensils!

5

A City Jungle of Different Sorts

L IFE IN THE city sustained a jungle of its own. Upon our arrival at the City of Mist we saw that everything remained the same as when we had left it. Old logging trucks drove slowly, carrying trees to who knows where. I wondered how many nests and birds might have been destroyed, and if trees were the only things they had removed from the forest.

"Mama, what are they going to do with all those trees?" I asked in fear that they had cut the forest entirely, leaving us with no nature or wildlife.

"They will build things for people," she replied.

With my childhood candor, I turned away from her thinking that trees must grow the same as flowers, not realizing that, for some of those precious trees, growth took over twenty years, if not a lifetime. We arrived first at *La Estación*, where old diesel buses came in and out and where commerce was the main source of income for most people. *La Estación* sold everything, from colorful and exotic birds to chained howler monkeys and nylon string mouth-shut iguanas. When I approached a monkey chained to a pole, his elongated arms swung at me as if asking for food, his large and watery eyes staring deeply into my own. Feeling hypnotized by his childlike stare and profound helplessness, I pulled Mama's skirt and asked her for money so that I could purchase the monkey and then set it free, but denying my request, she responded, "They will just sell more of those creatures."

I left with teary eyes, the monkey still staring from a distance. At that moment, I did not understand the spectacle I had just witnessed and felt saddened by it, unaware that someday, not too far away we too might become chained and endangered species. On our way home, we visited some stands to buy grains and foods. Always hungry, I had insisted on eating everything the food vendors offered in their wooden carts. In a corner, people lined up to purchase from a woman selling traditional *Vigorón*. Fixating my eyes and nearly salivating, I watched as her hands slowly placed crunchy pork rinds on a fresh banana leaf, topped the rinds with green cabbage salad seasoned with lemon juice or vinaigrette, salt and pepper, freshly sliced tomatoes and slowly-boiled yucca root. Meanwhile, Benjamin salivated like his city dog Skipper at the sight of sweet zapotes, sour jocotes and mouth-watering green mangoes. But reluctant as usual and suspicious to purchase food from the vendors, Mama refused to buy us the delectable treats offered at *La Estación*. "Look!" she said, pointing to one of the vendors in disbelief "She is handling money and preparing the meal at the same time!"

I agreed with Mama, the queen of sanitation, for she would only purchase food from people she knew and trusted. She had become exceedingly cautious about what we ate as she did not wish for the fate of Amanda to repeat. On the way home we followed Mama as she made several stops. She first visited the town's baker and began to speak with her friend Doña Autilia, who always complained of the calluses on her feet that were created by standing all day and by wearing hard-soled *caites*, durable sandals made out of cowhide. Meanwhile, we wandered around the bakery, curiously observing as the workers fed wood to oversized adobe ovens. The aroma of right-out-of-the-oven bread made our stomachs rumble while Mama made her purchase. Still, the hot bread did not make it into our mouths until later. Mama believed that hot bread gave people diarrhea.

Lastly, we visited Mama's godmother, La Madrina Trinidad, who lived about two long blocks away from home. After greeting her with hugs and kisses, Mama comfortably sat down and told her about our wildlife adventures one more time. Hungry and anxious to go home, we waited impatiently. Seven hungry children—who has the time to talk? My brothers and sisters asked to leave, but Mama's stare quickly placed them back in check. It was the way of life. People might have lacked wealth or freedom, but the commodity of time appeared to have been always available. And at last, we were home. Mama explained to Tatiana her planned dinner menu. My sisters and brothers ran to their bedrooms. Benjamin went inside the house, grabbed his wooden top and rushed outside to call neighborhood friends. I went to the garden to look for our turtle *Veloz*, Spanish for speed. *Tigresa*, our cat, had climbed on the roof. She had broken my trust when she decided to eat her own kittens, only because I touched them soon after they were born. Now, she missed my petting. Hairy Chilasta bugs guarded the fruit trees as they slithered up and down the tree trunks, waiting to burn any curious and trespassing human skin.

Outside, everything remained unchanged. The mists of the mountains still protected our town, at times casting an eerie feeling. Loose cobblestones revealed the dirt under the roads, and the church bell rang once every hour, three times to announce church services. People went about their daily routines, laughing and joking with the typical Latin American rhythm. Although life in the forest charmed my spirit, life in my provincial town also had magical trinkets of its own. Unusual characters gave the small town a unique character. Tatiana, our young and virginal helper, had a tale of her own to share. Although not a nun, she swore never to get married, as she knew too many undeserving men. And being the only remaining young girl in the house, I spent much of my time talking to Tatiana and following her wherever she went. To make her work more enjoyable, her job description also included watching over me. Running errands with her was amusing to me, although I had become the laughingstock to some of my uptight classmates, who thought that walking around town by her side gave me an undesirable reputation. I did not care. Tatiana was a beautiful person, spiritually and physically. Besides, the reward of mingling with the town's people and listening to their conversations could not be traded for selfish presumptions. After all, everyone had valuable things to offer regardless of their class status or beliefs. The shoeshine boy had the freedom to get dirty; the beggar had the freedom to be lazy, and the drunkard, the freedom to hallucinate.

I must admit code switching between the different classes was necessary and inevitable, as I would be forced to co-exist within both worlds. At school, I turned into a reputable and honorable young woman full of manners and Castilian vocabulary. In town, I became one of the ordinary people in being highly spirited; at home I became my true self, curious, loving and outspoken. The forest was another story: I became the liberated child of the wilderness, a helpless advocate for the endangered species and a witness of deforestation, who felt hopeless as the tumbling fall of trees made the ground tremble around me.

On a daily basis, Tatiana's routine began with a trip to the town's tortilla maker. Juanita possessed the reputation of the sweetest and most talented *tortillera* in town. Her short body and her round face always welcomed us with a smile. She created every tortilla carefully with her short and stout hands. Her overworked hands shaped every round scoop of corn dough with a systematic, careful and delicate process. First, she placed small ball-sized dough onto the palm of her hand. Clapping her hands together in a circular motion, she flattened the dough until it was perfectly proportioned. When she was done with this step, she placed the flattened dough on a hot *comal* and turned each tortilla until golden and puffed.

"Un córdoba," she requested smiling.

The freckles on her skin highlighted by the heat of the wood stove gave her, at times, a childlike face. She followed the same process for every tortilla she made. Stopping only to collect the money into her nearly-torn apron, she rinsed her hands in her stone sink and resumed, in harmony with her daily task. The tortilla routine never became old as I willingly volunteered to pick up the family's tortillas when Tatiana could not go. When no one watched, Doña Juanita allowed me to help her make a few, but resumed to her role after I had popped the bubbles on the tortillas too soon and made them look as if they had been chewed. My family had to wait patiently for me to return home with the tortillas as that outdoor kitchen, so humble and magical, absorbed me. The absence of walls and the chill of the trees waving their leaves did not seem to bother her as she always did her job with dignity. Every tortilla had a smile of Juanita imprinted on it. At one point, I seriously considered becoming a tortillera, if Mama would only allow it. When tortillas were not needed, sweet bread with a hot cup of coffee, or warm milk for the children, were in high demand. Following the daily noon siestas, Ernestina, our town's bread goddess, would appear, pacing steadily around her product, scenting the streets with the smell of warm, sugar cane sweetened bread.

On another day, I sat next to Mama outside our house as the town woke slowly to the daily one-hour-long traditional siesta. As the church announced 1:00 p.m. in its classical rhythm and the town resumed its normal activity, Ernestina strolled down the street to rescue me from my noon boredom, shouting, *"¡Pan Caliente!"* The shadow of her sun-kissed silhouette, in harmony with her movements, reflected how she expertly balanced an oversize breadbasket on her head. Moving her hips from left to right, her arms synchronized with her hips. The warm bread Ernestina sold pleased my senses each day, so holding a few córdobas in my hand, I rushed to greet her.

"*¡Aquí, Ernestina, Aquí!*" I said as I offered her money in exchange for that warm and aromatic bread. But before I could get my hands on that sweet piece of bread, two *chigüines* snatched a piece of bread from her basket and ran away. Ernestina then placed the basket back onto her head and began to chase after them.

"*¡Vengan aca sinvergüenzas!*" she yelled as she called back on two shameless boys who had stolen a piece of bread from her basket. Ernestina was not a woman to be easily fooled, and to show them the way things worked, she ran fast, pumping her legs up and down, all the while balancing the heavy basket on her head. Eventually catching up to one of the shameless boys, she pulled on his ear and demanded her money back.

"No one runs away from me," she admonished. Then resuming her normal posture, she walked back to us as if nothing had ever happened.

"*¡Cerrá la boca, niña!*" Mama said.

Not closing my mouth as directed, I stared with my eyes and mouth wide open, seeing Ernestina perform. It had been remarkable to see her chase after the boys with that basket perched on her head, carefree, as if forgetting she had it on.

"*¡Enséñame, Ernestina!*" I pleaded for her to show me how to balance the basket.

"Todo está en tu cabeza," is all I ever got from her.

Everything is in your head! I practiced placing my toys and kitchen pots on top of my head but with no success. After a while, I gave up and left that deserving role solely for Ernestina to fulfill. For years, Ernestina brought joy to our stomachs with her freshly-balanced bread, but after the so-called accidental death of her sixteen-year-old son, Ernestina and her sweet *pan caliente* never came knocking to our door again. Rumors spread that she followed her son to heaven, also by accident. Others implied she ran away to the coast—the coast of no return. We continued to sit outside our porch waiting for her as if she would come again. At times, I imagined Ernestina's sun-kissed silhouette appearing under the shadows of the sun. Mama would always greet any passerby that went by our house. Don Porfirio Callado often enjoyed sitting down with us, and he would lead an unrushed conversation about the town's latest goings on. Don Porfirio told Mama about the unfortunate and unclear accident of a farmer's son, the disgraceful pregnancy of Don Juan's daughter before reaching the altar, and the dreadful fate of dissidents as they claimed their rights. Dipping store-bought bread into my milk I savored my favorite whole grain *Cemita* bread, sweetened with brown sugar and molasses. I sat quietly, looking at the horizon, disengaged from the conversation as I indulged in my own enjoyment.

"Mama, will you be eating bread today?" I remembered to ask.

"I am not hungry," she replied.

"Please, eat some," I insisted.

As usual, she ignored the persistent pleadings of an insolent child. Begging Mama to join me did not work. Although almost anything could easily bring a smile to my face, bread especially did. However, as with so many other things in her life, it was unable to make Mama happy.

"They also found Miskito Indians, piled dead like a pyramid!" Don Callado continued.

"Tenga buen dia, Don Callado, " Mama retreated wishing him a happy day annoyed by the negative news Don Callado would often bring.

The day ended quietly as Mama prayed, read the Bible and we watched the daily television before bedtime. Our neighbors joined us at 7:00 p.m. daily to watch the popular *Novella,* as some of them did not own a television, or even if they did, adults enjoyed talking at the end of the episode about the antagonist's evil doings and the protagonist's ill-portrayed innocence. During that hour, everyone in the room appeared to adopt a character and drifted into dreams. Other than religion, the dramas of the Nicaraguan soap operas took people away, at least temporarily, from their daily troubles and tribulations, transporting them into worlds of romance, gossips and betrayals, unlike that of a terrorizing and fearful world a possible war threatened. As the sun would rise daily, a set of routines would follow, but rising in the morning was another story. Mama woke me and urged me to get ready for school by the crow of the rooster. I could hear the cowbell of the milkman as he went around the town delivering stainless steel canisters of fresh milk. Miguel would not come to our doorstep, as our milk would come from our farm.

Every night, I went to bed troubled by the mythical appearances of the haunting *Carretanagua*, as legend had it that she emerged during the late hours of the night. She haunted the dreams of Nicaraguans and was said to be a bewitched wooden cart that roamed the streets during the darkest part of the night, making crackling noises, instilling fear in people, and particularly in innocent children like me. Scared at the thought of *La Carretanagua*, I went to sleep with my head under my pillow and my bottom propped up. No doubt, fear had turned me into an ostrich. And there were many times I swore I heard *La Carretanagua* pass by my house.

"*¡Despierta mi niña!* My dear," Mama would whisper softly, urging for her little girl to wake up.

"*¡Un minuto mas Mama!*" I would beg for another minute.

"*¡No mas!*" Mama then would demand, refusing to give me more time to slumber. Every morning, Tatiana, too, came into my room and offered to finish what Mama had started. She entered the room and lifted me up from my bed. "*¡Levantate ya!*" she scolded.

"No!" I complained. Upsetting Mama and Tatiana each morning must have been one of my main roles as a child in that town, for waking me up would always be a struggle. Tatiana had to drag me out of bed and shove me into the shower while singing

Con sus calzones	With patched
bien remendados	up shorts,
Paso el patito	went the duckling
para la escuela	to school,
Iva cantando	He went on singing,
¡Viva la escuela!	Let the school live on!
¡Viva el maestro!	Let the teacher live on!
¡Y viva yo!	And let me live on!

I had prompted her to stop singing. *"¡Está bien!* I'm awake now, Tatiana!" I had cried as she quickly detangled my hair, struggling through every "ungodly curl," as she would often say.

"Mama!" I called out, displaying my few missing teeth.

"Shhh, quiet. I am done now. Go on and learn how not to give your mama a hard time in the morning," she chided softly as she was afraid of Mama. Eventually, we both gave up our fight and continued with our day.

Although attending school was supposed to be fun and exciting, personally it was more of an inconvenience, especially when it required waking up early and leaving our town dog Skipper behind.

Skipper was a type of mixed golden retriever, and even though he was officially Benjamin's dog, I knew he missed me very much, and I would miss him, too. Serving me well, Skipper wagged his tail as if to assure me that he would be there when I returned. By now, my three oldest brothers and two sisters had graduated from high school and were heading for college. The only ones left to endure elementary school were Benjamin and I, who were not particularly fond of it. My first day of school might have been similar to that of most children my age, although Mama had waited until I was a bit older. I cried and clung to my mother's skirt clueless of what awaited me at school. I felt frightened by the K-12 Catholic School ran by unyielding Spanish missionaries. The idea of becoming an exemplary, rule-abiding student gave me a lot of discomfort. Upon arrival, I saw that everyone looked the same. At El Colegio La Salle, boys and girls wore blue bottoms. Girls were dressed in pleated skirts and cotton shirts with a collar that had clear white buttons and the logo of the school embroidered onto the left pocket. Knee-high white socks complimented the outfit. The school officials would inspect our shoes for cleanliness as we walked through the school gate. Mama walked Benjamin and me on the first day of school but as soon as we were on school grounds, Benjamin reunited with his friends, and we separated. Inside the classroom stood my first Kindergarten teacher, Señorita Maria de la Caridad, holding a wooden ruler and analyzing my complexion with her small eyes and perfectly pulled-back hair. Although the ruler's role would be to point to the letters and numbers on the chalk board, something about the way she patted it on her hand while pacing herself around the room made me feel like a feral horse about to be tamed. *"Sentaté aquí,"* she ordered, instructing me to sit on a wooden desk. Feeling like an abandoned puppy, I waved goodbye to Mama as tears quietly escaped me. This moment became the beginning of awareness. It settled into my mind like an imprint on sediment. I would soon learn more than letters and numbers. I would learn the fact that being away from my family would become a way of life.

Mama's Nacatamales

First Dough
Approx. 2 cups water
(to desired texture)
5-6 cups corn dough
1 cup lard
Salt to taste
½ cup sour orange juice
4 cups chicken broth or powder
Bourbollin
1-2 teaspoons minced garlic
Cumin seeds

Second Dough
Approx. 1 cup water
(to desired texture)
3 cups corn dough
½ cup lard
2 cups chicken or beef
broth
sour orange juice
½ teaspoon minced garlic
a pinch of Achiote

YIELDS APROXIMATELY A DOZEN

Filling
¾ cup rice
2 cups chopped potatoes
1 chopped onion
Stuffed olives
2 chopped bell peppers
2 sliced tomatoes
Seasoned chicken, beef or pork
Peppermint leaves

Wrapping
Banana Leaves
Pre-cut banana and nylon
strings
Aluminum foil sheets
Lots of love and
PATIENCE!

Substitutions:
Achiote—Annatto Seeds or Paprika
Lard—Olive or Vegetable oil
Traditional dough—Store bought corn flour or corn meal
Patience—Nicaraguan Music such as Cumbias might help!
Love—No substitute!

6

Banana Leaves, Please!

A FTER ENDURING my first days of school, life carried on as usual, and Mama continued to nurture our growing appetite. One day, she asked me to run a quick and simple errand. She prepared the kitchen for her well-known Nacatamales, a dish made only for specific occasions: Christmas, New Year's, birthdays, and family gatherings or simply at Papa's request. This time there were two reasons: Papa's request and a family gathering, as all of my siblings had come home from college.

Mama's Nacatamales could not be imitated for she spent endless hours boiling and seasoning the corn dough. "Help me with the ingredients," she would instruct as she placed a large pot on the stove. Tatiana and I often took turns in assisting Mama. My favorite part was helping Mama prepare the dough. I assisted by first mixing the grounded corn dough with the chicken broth, the sour orange juice, a pinch of salt and cumin seeds, chopped onions, minced garlic, and the lard. Tatiana helped prepare the filling by chopping up onions, bell peppers, and potatoes, soaking the rice and seasoning the beef or chicken with salt and Achiote. Mama then began the grueling process of boiling the first dough until the dough reached Mama's desired texture. Her swollen feet supported her tired body as she stirred the dough once counter clockwise, and then twice clockwise relentlessly, adding the water and the broth gradually on low heat. Once she completed the laborious process of making the first dough, she then proceeded with the second dough while allowing for the first dough to cool. I handed her more chicken broth, water, salt, chopped onions, minced garlic, sour orange juice, lard and Achiote for coloring. Mama continued with the same process of stirring as she did with the first dough.

After Mama had spent hours standing like a hen, alternating one foot on the ground while resting the other, my other job was to bring home more store-bought banana leaves needed to complete the arduous task. I ran out of the house with intentions of doing what I'd been told, but urged on by my imagination, I went on swinging from tree to tree, wearing only banana leaves as I strolled through the

Nicaraguan rain forest in the company of my wild friends, my long-gone dog Ladrón, and my horse Lucero. I would dream day and night of this wonderful way of life. I turned out to be several beings living in one divine body, a butterfly transforming constantly through the different stages. During school breaks, I became a free-hearted jungle girl who loved our farm most of all where I rode my horse without restriction, swam in the spring pools, caught fireflies and other bugs, rolled down the green hills and stared at the large round eyes of the cows as I walked past them. However, during the school year, I transformed into a stiff and proper *señorita*—and it was this girl, who allowed me to get pinched by the mean daughter of the grocery store owner, Carlota.

"Banana leaves, please!" I had simply asked.

Handing me the banana leaves with one hand and pinching me with the other, cruel Carlota laughed as I ran away in tears. Angry with myself for allowing her bullying behavior, I swore to myself that I would return her favor the next time around. I arrived later than poor Mama had anticipated.

"Where have you been?" she asked.

"I became distracted and Carlota…"

"You and your fantasies need to stop! Life is real, Ileana." Mama cut me short.

Mama began to scoop a ball of the first dough onto a softened banana leaf, adding another ½ scoop of the red second dough, then topping it nicely with peppermint leaves, seasoned beef, chicken or pork, stuffed olives, rice, tomatoes, bell peppers and potatoes. To conclude her extravagant masterpiece, she wrapped each Nacatamal in more banana leaves, a sheet of aluminum foil and tied it like a gift with a dry banana or nylon string. Lastly, she placed each Nacatamal inside the boiling water pot. The Nacatamales boiled slowly for about four hours. The time they took to cook felt eternal to my rumbling stomach.

Family dinners were truly memorable and much anticipated by Mama since they now happened rarely with all of us at the table. This wholesome unity remained engraved into our hearts for the turbulent years ahead. Always the last one at the table, Mama made sure that everyone was satisfied. The rules of the table were clear: you could only speak when given permission, or when our turn came. Both Mama and Papa closely enforced table manners. At times I felt as if I belonged to a military base. While growing up, my parents taught me to communicate at all times, regardless of the situation. Papa always made me explain my reasons to him for anything and everything. If I wanted a toy, I had to explain why regardless of the obvious reason that I wanted to play with it. If I wanted a new pair of jeans, I had to explain that it was because I was growing and water puddles weren't as common in town as they were at the farm, therefore, my pants now needed to reach down all the way to my ankles. Eventually, I mastered the art of explanation and defense, and I succeeded at much higher rates than my siblings at getting what I wanted. At times I even became a mediator for my siblings' inefficient communication skills.

"Papa, Francisca could use a new pair of jeans. She looks tight in those, don't you agree?" I said, ignoring the rules imposed by my parents.

"Be quiet now or you will eat in the kitchen," he replied upset. He then stood up and walked over to where I was sitting. I closed my eyes tightly and waited for his wrath.

"You are never to advocate on behalf of someone else's affair again. Everyone must learn to stand on their own ground if one is to survive." He walked toward my sister and repeated; "You must learn to stand on your own ground if you ought to survive."

He waited for Francisca to acknowledge his words of wisdom and returned to his seat. Francisca's eyes became watery and everyone else remained quiet for part of the night. At last, Mama removed her apron, placed it on top of the kitchen chair and adjusted our painting of the Last Supper that had tilted. She joyfully joined us as if she had been oblivious to what took place. "You are all so grown," she said to my brothers, who had grown mustaches and beards. Ramon's Adam's apple moved up and down conspicuously as he ate and spoke, causing my attention to divert to his neck rather than my plate. I wondered if my brother had truly swallowed the forbidden apple as Mama had read in the Bible. Mama was right; my brothers didn't appear the same. Francisco's beard had grown past his chin, and he appeared much older. Papa, on the other hand, had skin softer than that of a baby. He preferred to keep a clean face. His cleft chin deepened each time he shaved with a sharpened knife that would slide smoothly through the pure soap lathered onto a bristle shaving brush. Benjamin broke the silence at the table as everyone began to laugh at the sight of him feeling his neck in search for his own Adam's apple, but to no avail, as he was still too young. That was a fantastic night, filled with enjoyment and old family memories. My older brothers and sisters recalled the times they were little and laughed at their reckless adventures, while Benjamin and I dreamed about growing up. We celebrated life and the growth of our loved ones, as is the natural thing to do in life. That night would have been an appropriate moment to have frozen in time.

7

The Year of Sulfur

"Mama, how do you know the devil is nearby?"
I asked one day.

"The devil smells like sulfur," Mama simply
responded.

THE YEAR of sulfur—1979—brought the
stench of the devil to our nation, or better yet,
my world. And children like me smelled sulfur for
the first time, up close, through the artillery that
instilled fear on the civilians of Nicaragua and the
faces of the dead that infiltrated our dreams. If only
we had known the future, we could have savored
every moment at our dinner together, for a little
longer. Unfortunately for me, I was born in a
country highly desired by a line of tyrants, which I
will leave for the history books to explain in detail.

History no doubt has the record straight when it comes to the bleeding of Nicaragua, and many well-known journalists have witnessed and written about it. Bleeding, due in part to foreign intrusions such as those of the Spanish Conquistadores, the Soviet Union, the abusive dynasty of way before my time—the Somoza Regime—and even the country which has now become my new home, the United States of America. To me, however, the only history that would come to matter as a child would be the one which began soon after I was born. Nicaragua, the strong lady of Central America, has repeatedly married rulers that misunderstood her assets, thus, bringing corruption, bloodshed and exploitation to her people and natural resources. In all of her marriages, she has endured minimum days of wealth for she engulfed herself in a turbulent and oppressive marriage of forty long years to the dynasty of the Somoza regime. According to some people, Anastasio, the first Somoza president who took power with the support of U.S. troops, had a modern vision for Nicaragua. Yet the corrosiveness of power and greed eventually took over as Anastasio "Tachito" Somoza Debayle, the second son of Anastasio Somoza Garcia and the last Somoza dictator, became flawed by corruption. He ended as the last ruler of a dynasty that lasted from 1936 to 1972, the year before my birth. The tumult-uous and overwhelming set of events and the continuous dispute as to which party would run the country, created yet another bloody and endless civil war as Contras revolutionaries, aided by the United States through the Iran-Contra deal, along with the confrontations by unrelenting Sandinista soldiers, devastated the country some more. The innocent citizens of Nicaragua, as always, ended up paying the high price, the merciless price of knowing when hell evolved but not when it would end.

"Share the wealth!" a liberalist claimed. He wore a red and black kerchief, as he rallied up the people to set up stages and barricaded the streets with piles of burning tires. The blue skies quickly turned grey as the heavy smoke rose up and the smell of rubber and oil became intoxicating.

"Leave our country, leave our land, and leave us free to decide!" they shouted.

They were upset; that I understood. Their cause became fueled by the patriotism of their past leader, Augusto Cesar Sandino, a farmer turned into a General who changed history and became the subject of study for Latin American history, the same young General who had spared my Abuelo's life years before my time and who was later betrayed and assassinated by Anastasio Somoza Garcia. General Augusto Cesar Sandino lived in the hearts of the Sandinista insurgents as a deity. His bravery and patriotism fueled their spirits and since his death, the Sandinista Front fought with more intensity. As the possible defeat of the Somoza regime became less of a dream and more of a reality, the young Sandinista revolutionaries stormed into the streets full of hopes and ambitions for their motherland, singing along with a song that played on a handheld radio, *"The Children of Sandino don't sell out, don't give in..."* Local newspapers released bold news of the soon-to-be defeated Somoza Debayle, creating more uncertainty among the people. Stories got repeated on the radios day and night about Somoza's soldiers fleeing from bloody battles and people talked about the same subject endlessly: Who won the battle today? How many died? What would become of the country and the people? Will we finally meet a fair government and enjoy freedom? What would it be? Who could it be? It was life changing; history in the making. From this point, the lives of many people were solely in the hands of God, as soon enough they began to lose whatever remained: their lives, children, and for vast numbers, even their dignity. Sitting on the front porch of the house while dipping rosquilla bread into fresh ground coffee, we hosted typical family reunions in the midst of endless war news and town happenings.

"The Sandinistas are accusing the National Guard of decapitating a soldier," the newspaper informed.

"The National Guard accuses the Sandinistas of assaulting landowners, raping women and cutting off their breasts," the alarming radio reported. And depending on the source of the news, the stories changed to accommodate the desired reactions.

"¡Los que pagan son los inocentes!" uncle Polín exclaimed as he walked into our house. He believed

the innocent were the bait that paid the highest price.

"¡Tio Polín!" I would shout while jumping onto his back when he arrived at our house. He traveled by horse and by public transportation; his farm was located farther into the forests than Papa's farm.

"How are my little calves?" he would ask, while tickling my brother and me with his rough and calloused hands.

When Tio Polín, Papa's closest brother visited, he often talked about the turbulence and the economy of the country. Papa tentatively listened, expressing growing concern about the war that might soon trail into our town. Remaining neutral and optimistic, they felt that the Somoza dynasty had ruled for too long and were hopeful that something positive might arise from the new Sandinista Government, as did the rest of the country. On the day of my uncle's arrival, an unusually quiet tone rendered throughout the town. From our house, questions were apparent on people's faces as they struggled to go unnoticed with their daily routines.

"Silence," they urged each other as the radio announced breaking news.

The atmosphere felt dense throughout the town. The sky became cloudy as mist spread slowly as if offering a warning of an unforeseen storm. The ominous shadow cast a curtain over the town, and silence sealed many tongues. At home, everyone in the room froze with anxiety as Papa and uncle listened to the radio. Heavy news of an unclear future nearly broke the radio's frequencies. The thickness of the air, preceded by the silence of the country, revealed a future that would later become a permanent dream in the memories of many. Who would have thought that many of the people in our country would soon become ex-landowners, ex-citizens of the country or ex-living beings? On every station they tuned to, news of the Somoza dictatorship ending was reported. For many hours, the radio would be the only thing heard in almost every household. Playing, while listening to the news coming from the neighbor's radio and my home as well, I learned about the corrupt dictatorship led by our president Somoza and the cruelty he had inflicted on so many citizens. Not comprehending politics well, and feeling uneasy, I continued to carve drawings on the ground with a stick. I even challenged myself to climb the highest point of a guanabana tree. Climbing to the top, and suddenly becoming aware of how far I had climbed, I screamed for help, *"¡Mama, Ayudamé!"* And rushing to my aid, poor Mama nearly tripped on the doorsill.

"Ay, *Chigüina,*" she scolded. "Francisco, come get this child down from the tree!"

Soon he came to my rescue and gave me his signature stare. His small, menacing eyes guarded by his long eyelashes fixated on me as he figured out how to solve the problem quickly. The only solution was for him to climb and hold my hand as we slowly came down together.

"Can't you see we are busy?" he complained.

One minute, or even a second, however meaningless it may appear, can make a tremendous difference on anyone's future. I enjoyed the minute of attention my brother gave to me and the safety of his strong grip, but I was not aware of what that minute meant to him or the country. I was not aware of the changes the transient passage of time might bring to his life and into the luxury of a worry-free childhood. Unable to go to sleep that night, I decided to search in the kitchen for a late snack. At first, the brightly-lit fireflies and the melody of the crickets and frogs outside sidetracked me. Then I noticed two mysterious silhouettes in the dark. Sitting in the patio, under the shelter of obscurity, my parents spoke of the uncertain future ahead.

"What will happen?" Mama questioned.

"We'll have to wait and see," Papa answered.

Their voices had a frightening tone. My mind twirled with endless questions I knew might never be answered, and my heart rate rose at the thought of losing any of my loved ones. Rumors, tragedy, and unfortunate events spread quickly throughout town. Don Domitilo ran into a land mine and vanished without a trace. Don Clemente disappeared with the bewitched Següa, never to be seen again. Don Pedro said too much and died by accident as he fell head first onto a rock; a week later, his son, too, got lost in the forest—a wild cat might have eaten him alive. And so it went, all deaths resulted from criminal luck and accidental calamities.

The following day everything proceeded as usual. Tío Polín returned to his home in the forest. After him came Papa's youngest brother Tío Ysidro, who had come to seek psychiatric help for his youngest daughter. Unlike Tío Polín, Tío Ysidro saw life from a serious perspective and treated his children harshly, ridding them of the rightful fantasy of childhood. He treated his children as adults and denied them the gift of education and play. He trained them to work and earn their living as soon as they began to walk, like a farmer trains his mule. The children worked for their father and were expected to die caring for him. Nevertheless, just as it is true for many of us, what we wish for isn't always what we get.

May 20, 1979. Ill-omened clouds whirled in the sky; the thick air made it hard to breathe as changes were brought upon our small town. It had been decided that the last Somoza president, Anastasio Somoza Debayle, would soon be overthrown by the FSLN (Frente Sandinista de Liberación Nacional.) It was early in the morning. I cannot remember the exact time for all I can remember is the feeling of disorientation as we awoke to the thunderous sound of an explosion from a field right across from our house.

"Earthquake!" shouted Mama as the explosion made the ground shake. We all ran around the house in circles. Soon after came the shivering sound of the Red Cross siren ordering us to evacuate our homes. Using loudspeakers, they instructed us to grab only our basic belongings and head towards refuge. Still in disbelief, we ran outside to see what was going on and this was the first time that the smell of sulfur nearly scarred my nostrils. I could see and smell the sulfuric air left by the bomb. Our town was under attack. We could hear gunfire exchanges beginning to take place in the surrounding areas of the town. Since 1963, the guerrillas led by Sandinistas had become tired of the Somoza regime and slowly but surely were crawling from the mountains where they hid for so long into the nearby towns. They began a diligent uprising campaign that would eventually lead to the defeat of the Somoza dynasty.

"Hurry, you only have a few minutes," one of the priests urged Mama. Not knowing which way to go, the wind of change made us spin in circles, confused and disoriented. Unsure of what to do and still too young, I grabbed an old doll from the floor and clung onto Mama's skirt. Nothing makes a child mature faster than war. Mama grabbed whatever was at hand, and then rushed outside the house, nearly dragging my brother and me in desperation.

Mama often recalls how strongly we clung to her and did everything she told me. But eventually, I broke into tears of terror after seeing the stampede of people rushing towards the hills, some carrying their children on their shoulders, others dragging them, while a few left them behind, forgotten temporarily over the dominance of fear. Other than the annual procession of our Holy Mother Mary and festive town parades, I had not experienced such a large crowd: a multitude of people pushing and shoving each other frantically in the hope of moving just a few yards ahead. "It'll be all right," Mama assured us while gripping us with her cold and trembling hands. Somehow that cold feeling of her hands remained in my mind for years to come. The look on her face as she turned from one direction to another showed me the panic I had sensed when I had heard my parents speaking softly under the moonlight. Trembling with fear, I somehow managed to keep up with Mama, clinging to her closely. This was the first time I floated in the air.

"Where are Papa and my brothers?" I cried.

"They'll be here soon, my love!" she said, "Hush now and keep walking. I can't believe that coward Ysidro ran away without us," Mama cursed.

Tio Ysidro had been visiting with us for about a week then, along with his youngest daughter Lucida who had been diagnosed as emotionally disturbed. But upon the first sound of the siren, Tio Ysidro flew to seek refuge, forgetting entirely about his daughter and the rest of us, something our courageous Tio Polín would never have done.

Following the commands of the Red Cross, everyone walked quickly and in order up the hill towards the reputable *Colegio Sagrado Corazón de Jesus*. The fog appeared denser that day—but not dense enough to make us all disappear into its embracing mist. Rather, like frightened school-children following their teacher, we followed our parish priests who wore their white cassocks and gold crucifixes. They held a white flag tied up to a wooden pole up high as a symbol of peace. Meanwhile, hovering above us, were the warplanes of the National Guard impatiently allowing the Red Cross to finish the evacuation process so that they could begin the inevitable aerial bombardment of our town. The crowd ran to our refuge as the shootings and eerie sounds of war were catching up to us. At one point Mama must have dragged us; all I could feel was numbness and a heartbeat faster than my legs. Once we—the lucky ones—reached our refuge, the shiny stone floors of *El Colegio Sagrado Corazón de Jesus* welcomed us, irrespective of whether anyone had paid tuition or not. The religious school offered us shelter in its sterile classrooms. We were led to a room on the second floor that had large glass windows facing the outside. Mama hurried to take a corner and quickly began to make the cold floors comfortable with whatever blankets she had grabbed on the way out. Mama tried desperately to make the cold floors and the small corner feel like home. My cousin Lucida trembled and spoke continuously without making sense. I stood alongside my brother Benjamin by the glass window, witnessing with awed curiosity as the sky changed from grey hues to what appeared to be colorful fireworks.

"Fireworks!" We pointed and exclaimed in awe, but the adults in the room didn't care to even blink.

"They're dropping lights!" shouted Benjamin again with his eyes wide-open.

Thunderous explosions followed the array of fireworks, and we could see through the clear windows the people who were left behind running desperately towards the refuge where I stood. In my adult years, I once asked a psychologist and a friend of mine why some of us are cursed with a few unwanted memories, which never leave our minds, while new ones could easily disappear. She explained that our memory bank permanently seals memories that have a deep impact on our lives. I understood then that there would be no greater impact on a person's life than to come across the dizzying faces of death—the immeasurable damage humans are capable of. There was a man, a civilian running behind the crowd. He appeared to have been shot in his back. Other men threw their own bodies on top of their families in the hope of sparing their lives. Their bodies were lifted up into the air by the rain of bullets that fell from the skies…and so we fled away from the window to cuddle close to Mama and our absentminded cousin Lucida instead. My mind did not know how to process what I'd seen at that time; instead my heart appeared to do so as its accelerated beating didn't cease for a long while. That night Benjamin earned a fever as he was older and learned that those fireworks were more than awe-inspiring displays of lights. Everyone in the room appeared disabled by fear and no one spoke. The chatty Nicaraguans I was used to listen to since I was born no longer had much to say and they no longer smiled. We shared a room with many of the townspeople. Most could not sleep, but the few that gave in forced Lucida and me to contain our laughter from all the escaping noises they made. Mama prayed incessantly with the intonation of a preacher, and those that remained awake joined in the prayers. The prayers began as easy as Ave Marías and turned into unrecognizable sounds of strange tongue dialects. At no other time does religion become more consoling than when your life depends on miracles alone.

"Mama, I need to use the restroom!" I said with hurried anxiety.

"Don't wander off," she warned, immediately resuming her prayers. Our room felt the quietest amid the chaos as Mama's prayers appeased the broken spirits.

On my way to the restroom I became distracted by the sight of overcrowded classrooms, people huddling on the floor close to each other, infants crying due to the lack of milk and nuns rushing in and out of the classrooms in search for food and supplies. In the commotion, I strolled through hallways unnoticed and wandered further into the nuns' quarters. Rumors had spread that their rooms were sanctuaries that civil eyes should not see. To my disappointment the rooms were remarkably unsophisticated to the standards of a material world for the only object of admiration would be a crucifix that hung above the bed's headboard. The rooms were empty as all of the nuns were serving God. Therefore, upon my arrival at the restrooms, I came upon flooded wet floors, leaking toilets, lack of toilet paper, and worse, a long line of people waiting to take their turns. "Let the child go first," a kind lady said. I hurried through the first door that opened, soon realizing I was trapped inside the stall. I panicked.

"Un momento," a woman advised as she attempted to open the door.

The minute requested by the woman felt perpetual to me, so I impatiently squeezed under the thin space below the door, ignoring the water mixed with bodily fluids leaking from the toilet. The smell of urine-infected waters made me gag, and I held my breath until I was able to get out. The women outside stared at me with disgust and I ran away with my face reddened by the embarrassment and the stench of urine.

"¡Ave María Purísima!" Mama became distressed, and as I tried to explain my predicament, she stripped my dirty clothes off me, using only the privacy of an expanded blanket. The only bag Mama had managed to bring, which contained

130

everything but food, served its purpose. Mama pulled out a blanket, clothes and a bottle of castor oil and hurriedly scrubbed the urine-infested water off my body, removing the unpleasant odors. Meanwhile, my cousin Lucida remained absent, making only "apu, apu," sounds while pointing her fingers up in the air.

"What is wrong with Lucida?" I asked.

"She just needs someone to play with," Mama suggested.

"Lucida!" I called to her, "Do you want to play with my doll?" And without a response, Lucida simply yanked the doll from me and began to play. She played for hours, and the remaining days, with my old doll beneath the thunder of bombs, the torrents of bullets and the whispers of wind-blown cries, but my doll was never returned. My cousin just needed attention and a classic toy to cure her emotional disease. One of fifteen siblings, she became affected by my uncle's tight wallet and distorted theories.

"Toys are useless!" he would say, never allowing his children to dream beyond their day-to-day work routines.

After a while, we children adjusted quickly to the sounds of artificial thunder as Mama and the other fervent roommates put our lives in the holy hands of our forgiving father Jesucristo, and our blessed mother María. Resonating blast of bombs crushed the streets and heavy machinery annihilated homes and human bodies. The heart-pounding reverberation of people's fear now serenaded our lives. My own heartbeat increased to levels I was unused to. People murmured about images of red hues from mutilated corpses, missing body parts, and scattered guts that tainted our streets. And after the thunders of weaponry had ceased and there was no one else to kill, the tenebrous siren once again instructed us to resume our journey back home—as if nothing had ever happened. The frightened crowd gathered their belongings and cautiously stepped out of the building like deer into an open meadow. Slowly, people resumed their walk into town, but this time silence transpired through the multitude and no one shoved or hurried to get ahead, casting an eerie feeling among us. The clean smell of the air we were used to became replaced by the suffocating odor of gunpowder and a rusty smell of blood, along with a stench of burnt flesh like what we got when Mama burnt the skin of pigs at the farm. At that moment, I believed we had all gone to hell as described in the Bible burning in the flames of hell for all eternity. Mama held us by our hands; squeezing us so tight that we nearly lost blood circulation in our hands. From above the descending hill, we could see that the main road that led into the town had lifted from the ground by the bombing and the heavy war tanks; the once flirtatious cobblestones became scattered and dismantled. Smoke covered the sky and the destruction of the town was immeasurable. The rumors we had heard before from people and the news about the same happening in other places throughout the country had also become our reality. The closer we approached, the faster everyone moved and upon arriving, everyone scattered in hymns of despair. No one knew what to expect, or perhaps no one was prepared for what our eyes would witness next.

"*¡Dios mio, ten misericordia,*" bemoaned a distressed woman begging God for mercy as she held a severely injured young man in her arms. The poor man hung onto his last seconds of life; his interior had turned into his exterior. And he eventually let go as the Good Samaritan imprinted the sign of the cross onto his head.

"Papa, Mama!" wailed unattended children as they had been separated from their bewildered parents. The children like Benjamin and me were horrified. We could not distinguish reality from fantasy. And all we could do was cry while holding our heads and vomiting at the overwhelming rivers of blood that ran through the streets. I can only tell you that feeling of nausea lingers for a while. Much of this as I recall at this moment returns to my mind in the form of tasteless nightmares and distant memories, but every now and then I still seem to experience the heaviness on my feet as they refuse to move, the sinking of my stomach and the tightness on my throat that leads to an occasional loss of breath.

As expected in war, not everyone made it to the safety of the refuge. An injured soldier groaned with immense agony next to civilians who had failed to escape. Some lay there paralyzed by the loss of a leg or an arm, or were slowly bleeding to death. The rest were either dead physically or spiritually and they no longer held any expression on their faces. Benjamin, Mama and I held onto each other's hand. I stood quiet, unable to utter a single word and became overwhelmed while staring at paramedics who hurriedly carried the dead and the barely alive in whatever means were available: wheelbarrows, wooden planks, and even nylon sacks tied together. I thought it was a dreadful nightmare and waited for it to end, to be allowed another chance to awaken by my sweet Mama's side and by the mooing sound of cows, the roaring of jaguars, the chirping of birds and the caressing aromas of hidden orchids. I even wished to be pinched again by mean Carlota—that for sure would wake me up. As expected, I never woke up, and the nightmare continued its cataclysmic course. Forgetting that I stood beside her, my shaken Mama continued to tour the city in disbelief along with a disorientated multitude of people. She had become a missionary along with the priests, assisting and offering a last prayer to those who were dying. All the while Benjamin and I were becoming numb like the dead. Luckily for Benjamin, he could sprout out tears to ease the overwhelming fright, not me. Instead, the knots in my throat only tightened up more, causing my heart to ache and my ears to clog.

For the first time, I saw the dead up close, bodies lying on the streets, splintered body parts, springs of blood flowing through the crevices of the broken road, grown-ups crying like children, cars crushed by the heavy war tanks and houses destroyed and set ablaze. And to make matters worse, I saw the tasteless looting of whatever homes or businesses remained in place. We stood there as children, holding Mama's cold and bloody hands as we witnessed the transferring of dead and injured soldiers to and from my school. El Colegio La Salle had served as a temporary morgue. And it was then and for the first time that I understood that we also would disappear into the wind like dust. At that moment, we had become dust—weightless and unstable. The first gust of rotten luck had infiltrated my life, as I was to grow up in a war-stricken nation to be followed by a perilous future. These new lamenting cries echoed throughout our once quiet and misty valley. My eyes had seen too much. My brother and I had seen up close, as we held onto Mama's skirt, the emotionless and solemn faces of death. The dumbstruck faces of the surrounding adults shocked me at times more than the dead. I trembled as the innocence and dreams of children dissipated into the mist, and we no longer feared the Headless Rider or the Bewitched Carretanagua carriage, for we had become involuntary children of war. And although we were not 'children soldiers' like many other unfortunate ones, we had become nonetheless, children of war. Our senses had been exposed to sounds our ears were not accustomed to, the curtain in our eyes of sweet childhood had revealed the tainting of blood and our sense of smell could relate to our palates the iron-like taste of blood at the sight of fresh carnage, which, to make matters worse, attracted hovering *Zopilotes.* The bald-headed vultures circled in slow and somnolent motions over the clouded skies. They had gone crazy over the overwhelming smell of rotten flesh and the human feast being offered to them. How I came to detest those preying birds. The Red Cross cleared the streets, one dead or injured person at a time. Most of the dead were burned with gasoline on the streets, as there was no time for proper burials and to prevent diseases.

The fragility of life came upon the people of City of Mist. From that day on, adults could not stop venting about what they had seen, but chided us children to play while refusing to hear our own war stories. Had they forgotten we were there, too? Our dolls played victims, nurses and heroines while plastic cars turned into war tanks and plastic figurines into soldiers. It was how we, the children of war, told our stories, through the detailed recounts of our explicit plays. No doubt children hold a certain resilience adults should often adopt.

July 19, 1979. At last, after the life-shattering episode that had altered our simple lives, news spread rapidly that the Sandinista Front had finally defeated the Somoza regime. The glory of the long awaited defeat brought feelings of an inexplicable magnitude to Nicaraguans. People felt compelled to dream, laugh and hope for a better future based on true democracy and equality for ALL. And singing the new Sandinista slogan, the new government officials marched on the streets raising their red and black flags as a sign of victory.

Adelante marchemos compañeros,	Let's march compatriots,
avancemos a la revolución	into the revolution ahead.
Roja y Negra bandera nos cobija	Red and black flag cuddles us.
Patria libre!	Free Nation!
Vencer!	Win!
O Morir!	Or die!

Singing a new patriotic song I did not quite comprehend, and bringing closure to perhaps one of the biggest battles recorded in the history of Nicaragua, victorious chants echoed through the wind in honor of the fallen that had become a sinister evidence of a heroic cause. It was indeed the end of the Somoza dynasty and everyone cheered at the hope of a democracy, the type enjoyed in remarkably few nations: freedom to express without the fear of retaliation or repression, freedom to dream and keep your family together with choices beyond that of rationalized food and plastic sandals for all.

However, the bleeding land needed to hold onto her dream a little longer for our new and feisty government needed a chance to allow the sprouting of a new Nicaragua—a moment long awaited by the resilient Nicaraguans. But the bloody war was not yet over, for it was only the beginning. The peaceful world we were born to love intertwined in the silks of the mist, the melodies of the wild and the serenity of its exotic fauna, descended to the second place in our lives. We now quivered time and time again by one abrupt explosion after another. And every time the ground trembled and we heard the sounds of the siren, we ran inside the house traumatized and numb again. We lay flat on the floor, trembling like leaves and awaiting our fatal end. Reverberating explosions, whistling sounds of bullets and war tanks that threatened to break the ground replaced the usual tranquility with fear laced through our bodies. The first explosion outside our refuge felt like an earthquake as the detonation made the ground shake, but then we saw smoke and heard Mama calling for us to come with her to the room in the back of the house. Once in the room, we all hugged and lay on the floor waiting for the next bomb to fall upon our house. After a while, everything became silent. At that moment, silence was more frightening than sound as we could not anticipate what would come next. We waited a long time in silence and terror as our teeth ground against each other uncontrollably. You could hear the igniting whistle of what might have been a mortar and the short silence in between before it reaches its destination and explodes. The silence in between is what really takes away your breath, as no one knows for sure where it might land. When we decided to exit the room slowly, we crawled our flattened bodies through the house, pulling our upper body with our upper arms and carefully lifting our heads to look outside the window. When our neighbors went outside, we rushed to follow them. We should have stayed inside the house as the impressions of previous carnage exhibitions still eclipsed my mind. The Sandinista victory did not come uncontested, for a new revolution sprouted with U.S.-aided Contra revolutionaries.

Under our new threatened government, Nicaraguans now had the right to vote as long as no one found out they voted or became victims of calumny. Social classes reconciled as everything from food and clothing became rationalized and uniformed. We lined up to receive our portions of rice and beans, one bar of soap per family, one cereal box and neutral-colored plastic sandals for the entire family. No one was entitled to have more than others; not even the children belonged to their parents any more for if they were needed, they would then serve in the fight against the Contra revolution. But above all, there was hunger, misery and terrible fear.

After a while, things resumed to what some people considered 'normal.' I returned to the school where the ghosts of war guarded its gates and tainted its ground. And although the town was cleared and bodies were no longer exposed, somehow the smell of rusted blood remained, not to mention the haunting pictures that intruded into our thoughts and dreams.

"You are going to school," Mama demanded.

"No!" I cried, "I don't want to go!" Mama then held me tightly against her chest and repeated, "You must go to school!"

Dropping my body on the ground, I begged endlessly for Mama not to take me there. "Please, no!" I continued to cry while reaching over to my dog Skipper. Exhausted by my kicking and screaming, Mama eventually picked me up and carried me to school.

"She'll be fine, just let her stay," my new stern teacher insisted. "Soon she will learn to adapt!"

Crying and reaching towards Mama as she left me behind, I continued to scream. A few moments went by, and I detested the slow but unrelenting movement of the clock. I continued to cry for a while. Images of the dead people I saw who had been brought into the school filled me with uncontrollable terror. And finally after an exhausting period of sobbing, the school bell rang, and the happiest moment at school came: Recess! Instructed to go and play at the playground, I ended instead staring at the distance toward the roof of my house. I could hear Skipper barking, and I called out to him in desperation.

I wanted to go home, so I pressed my body against the fence. Not bothered by my wailing, the other children continued to play on the swings, on the tires and the slides. I could see them pointing towards me and laughing. At last I crawled under a small hole beneath the fence and crossed the street recklessly without looking to either side. Luckily, traffic was just an occasional event in our town and I ended safely in the sweet comfort of my home and the company of Skipper.

"*Niña*, what am I going to do with you?" complained poor Mama.

Lifting me up again, she returned me back to school, where I was welcomed with a hateful stare from my teacher. Clinging onto Mama's skirt, I held on and refused to stay. Mama, exhausted and embarrassed, finally gave in and took me back home with her. She tried to force me back the next day and for the rest of the week, but to no avail. I won the battle, I thought. Following several arguments with Papa, Mama decided to enroll me instead at the prestigious, all girls' school run by nuns, far away from the traumatic scenes that took place at *El Colegio La Salle*. Deep in her heart, she was doing what any loving mother would do, taking the necessary steps to ensure her child's well being. Therefore, unable to find an excuse not to attend, I dressed in a new and stricter uniform.

"Tighten her hair," Mama instructed Tatiana. "Re-iron her shirt, and make sure that her bow is in place."

Mama inspected every part of my body carefully and attentively. Up by 6:00 am and dressed nicely in my perfectly creased and pleaded skirt, white shirt with a tie, white stockings and shiny leather black shoes, I headed to my new school. For a moment, I felt like one of Papa's cows that were taken to the slaughterhouse. He checked and weighed the cows meticulously, ensuring that he would get his money's worth.

"Odd comparison," Mama said when I expressed my feelings, and then she added laughing as we went out the door, "Don't worry! You will be the cutest cow at school today."

She showed me the long route to school as we walked together up the hill towards the misty mountains. Mama talked about her first day of school. Learning new things excited her. In her excitement, she also shared a story. "Once, my school made a mistake with my grades and gave my high grades to the worse student at the school, and I received his failing grades. Upset, I ripped the report card in the principal's face, and in front of the entire school. I was suspended, and my parents were embarrassed and infuriated," Mama recalled. I was shocked by such confession and such familiar characteristics, but still worried about what was to become of me without Mama and my dog nearby. Located by the entrance of the city and nestled by mountains, El Colegio Sagrado Corazón de Jesus greeted me, only this time the classrooms that had been dismantled during our refuge were filled back with pupils' desks. Welcoming me to the Heart of Jesus Christ, my new school vowed to turn decent girls into self-sufficient, law-abiding citizens and, eventually, exemplary wives. At first, I felt intimidated by its size, the surrounding iron gates and glass windows all around, some of which faced directly onto a newly-acquired military station, but my nerves relaxed as we followed the tranquil lush gardens behind the locked gate. Somehow, the gardens softened the threatening outer shell of the building. La Madre Superiora waited by the shiny tile entrance, standing flawlessly rigid on her head-to-toe gray attire. The Superior Mother smiled gently and inspected me with a penetrating stare that automatically made me say, "Sí Madre." Crucifixes and images of our Holy Father gave me spiritual peace and assured me that my new school would be clear of any war ghosts.

"I'll take her from this point," the Superior Mother offered, holding my hand and guiding Mama politely to the exit.

Mama gave me a short kiss on my forehead, and whispered into my ear that I would be all right and that she would be waiting for me after school by the gate. With teary eyes, but feeling too scared to cry, I waved goodbye to her, who seemed teary as well, and followed the nun to my new classroom. It only took a couple of minutes for me to become acquainted with my new reality. Holding a wooden ruler firmly with her aged, sun-spotted hands and standing with a perfectly straight back, my new teacher, La Señorita Inpura, introduced herself to me and appeared no different than the bullying schoolmaster from the previous school. I have to admit, I was scared of her. Back home, I told Mama what I had observed, recalled her wrinkled and unfriendly face and compared it with the antagonist of a story Mama read to me that night.

The story portrayed an unmarried woman with a dry and wrinkled face that owned a bird, which sang magnificently every morning. The bird was a beautiful, fragile canary that sang songs of freedom, love and nature. But one day the bitter woman could not take his singing anymore and decided to end the noise by cutting out the canary's tongue. I detested the antagonist of the story for what she had done to the poor bird, but praised the beautiful canary for never giving up, because, even though his tongue had been removed, the bird still sang silent songs that resonated in the movements of his beak. Mama explained that the moral of the story was, "It doesn't matter what anyone takes away from you; the only thing they cannot take away is your soul. You go on my child and sing to the world if you wish, regardless of whether they cut your tongue as they did that of the beautiful canary. But you must try to prevent it so that other people can delight themselves with your beautiful songs." Smiling, Mama closed the book and kissed me goodnight.

"Why can't you teach me instead?" I whined.

"It's different, *mi niña*," she said as she prepared my uniform for the next day. "You need to go to school, just like other children, so that you can retell me new stories."

It was not until later that I identified with the poor canary of the story which, although silenced to sing, never stopped singing. Perhaps my destiny would be similar, and I was to become the human canary that would sing the story of an erstwhile paradise for the world to hear, in the name of those forever silenced throughout the world.

In a few days, I became well acquainted with my new school and its rigid conventions. The rules were straight-forward for most traditional town children: say yes to everything my schoolmasters and the nuns instructed and stand firmly in line with a straight back, chin up and with a dignified posture—the way a civilized lady ought to behave. No climbing of trees, no objections, no suggestions, no expressing of the mind and no questioning of authority. For a child who was never free to ride a horse, climb a tree, or get dirty playing with animals, or for one who was never allowed to join in adult conversations, such rules would probably not pose difficulty. I, however, got off on the wrong foot. I immediately forgot the rules and climbed a tree overlooking the town and my house. Therefore, I obtained my first after school detention. Meanwhile, waiting after school by the gate, sat Mama worried about what an awful thing I had already done.

"She climbed a tree during recess forgetting that she is a lady wearing a skirt," the upset nun explained.

Not surprised at my behavior, Mama said to her, "She will not do it again, Superior Mother." Pleased with Mama's response, the nun closed the gate behind us, and we walked home. Mama's submission upset me, and I accelerated my walk to be ahead of her. I could tell by the look of the Superior Mother that it was in her agenda to tame me as if I were a wild horse. However, after hearing Mama's many frustrated pleas, I finally agreed to make her happy. For the next few years, I made sure my posture became well defined and my manners were flawless, but my attitude towards and love for the trees and overall nature remained as tempting and inviting as ever. I learned appropriate penmanship and reading skills. I was educated in music, mathematics, art, science, cooking, etiquette, crocheting, embroidery, history and religion, the holy readings of the Bible, prayers for mass, and the history of all the heavenly saints of the Catholic Church.

However, despite my high academic achievements and unrelenting effort to become an exemplary citizen, earning detentions and punishment at that school was easier than breathing. On a day when the nuns were in a good mood, "Twenty: I will sit or walk straight standards." On an inauspicious day, whenever I was not displaying proper posture, the wooden ruler would touch my skin. I served after school detention if my uniform did not appear ironed to perfection, regardless of whether I tried to convince the teacher that Tatiana had ironed it, as I was still too young. I served detention for not lining up on time, and for daydreaming while in class: it was school suspension if I spoke my mind in any way. I have to confess that I earned a few of those and as a result I added to Mama's premature graying process.

8

Las Griterias

ONE MUST sacrifice even the dearest things in life in order to obtain the privilege of freedom, for freedom rarely ever comes free. For a while, things almost resumed their normal course. Mama and Papa continued to argue over his new forbidden romance and the latest broken fence at the farm. My brothers and sisters went back and forth from home to college and in Francisco's case from home to the mandatory cotton fields' pickings and back to college. It was there that the calluses on his hands, obtained at the farm while wrestling bulls and taming horses, came to benefit as he was not given gloves to pick the cotton and the thorns nearly ripped his hands apart. Benjamin and I had no worries yet and we played endlessly with disagreements, finally ending our games with a push and a bruise here and there. But upon returning from school one day, sobbing and praying for a miracle, I found Mama kneeling on the floor in her room, arms up in the air towards the image of Jesus Christ. She begged persuasively for my brothers to return to her arms safely.

"Mama, what's wrong?" I asked, confused about her behavior.

"They're taking my boys," she cried in despair.

We heard the sound of the military trucks and rushed outside. Mama nearly crushed my hands as we stood by the roadside witnessing the violation of mothers' hearts that was taking place without impunity. Except for the previous human carnage, City of Mist had never appeared gloomier. The day of the feared mandatory military draft that was implemented by the Sandinista Front had arrived. Like a malign disease, it had come knocking to our doors taking young boys the state deemed old enough from the safety of their nests. The soldiers stormed inside homes with their camouflage uniforms and black combat boots. They pulled children, not yet men, from their mothers' arms and threw them inside open army trucks, to pursue an unclear cause that not many of them lived to retell. They then drove the boys to a vague destination, a clandestine base where they received a few days of training, if at all, and were then shoved into combat with tears in their eyes and fear controlling their minds. "They have taken my three children to become *carne de cañon*!" Mama had said, when unprepared boys served as meat for the cannons. The soldiers trampled them if they refused, beating and dragging them into the trucks. Mama held onto Carlo's shirt and was nearly dragged along with him but was released swiftly by one of the soldiers who pulled her arm and threw her onto the ground. I followed Mama and my brothers, crying as my heart filled with impotence. Benjamin also cried and even tried kicking one of the soldiers, but upset and laughing, the soldier pushed him on the chest with his rifle and told him to wait for his turn. Mama knew that the only chance of survival my young brothers had was the hard labor and discipline Papa had instilled in them while at the farm. Other than that, they only possessed strong dreams, dreams that kept my family human, pursuing our lives with dignity, regardless of the perils that came our way. We had dreams to love and to be loved and dreams to achieve extraordinary things. Making a positive difference became the ultimate dream, as humans that escaped the number line. In a country like ours, dreams tend to become as indispensable as oxygen and water, a forced necessity, not a commodity.

Feeling helpless, I squeezed Mama's hand tightly as we stood on the curb for I did not know what else to do. Her face flooded with tears, and I could barely see her small honey eyes. I struggled to utter magical words to calm my suffering Mama but nothing came to mind. At that moment, I was just a useless child—I had become my mother's shadow. A vast sadness and helplessness knotted my throat, blocking my words. The only thing my body should have allowed were tears to flow freely, as they were the only things that could represent my sympathy. But I could not even do that. Again, I stood still and motionless as Mama shook my hands from hers and joined the screaming mothers up the main cobblestone road and after the green muddy trucks. The soldiers teased the women by pointing at them with their rifles and towards their young sons, but at that moment nothing seemed to matter. I ran behind Mama. I thought for sure the soldiers would shoot at them as they were cursing the soldiers. The new resilient Nicaraguan mothers, once sweet and abnegated, had turned into fearless lionesses.

Once my brothers were out of sight and many desperate mothers, including my own, gave up running after the military trucks, the sobbing citizens returned to their homes filled with dread. Mama appeared thinner than ever, while Papa sat quietly outside the house, pretending to be in much more control than she was, but his trembling lips and the weighted look of his shoulders signaled that his attempt at being calm was a lie. For a man like him, to express such emotions meant creating another deep sorrow within. In an effort to help my inconsolable Mama, he said, "Our boys will be fine! They are strong. Do your prayers and ask God to help us." He said while hitting the ground with a rusted machete used to trim the shrubs. Then placing her hands together up to the sky, Mama pleaded to God once more for the nightmare to end.

On a sad day like that, playing did not appeal to me. Benjamin pretended to play with his cars as he pushed them back and forth along a track in the dirt road he had traced in the ground. Unsure of what to do, I sat high up in a mango tree overlooking the winding road to see if I could spot the trucks that took my three musketeers away. Mama and Papa looked at Benjamin with despair and frustration at the thought that one day his turn might come. Only shortly absorbed into the pain, I returned to do what children do best. As a child, I unconsciously learned to block reality with the innocence of my childhood and although I attempted to make sense of my surroundings, I naturally resumed what some consider a normal routine. It didn't take long before a beautiful butterfly teased me with her colorful wings that opened and closed, and I climbed down from the tree and began to chase after it.

As usual, I became preoccupied with my own paradise, surrounded by forests, rain, my turtle Veloz, my cat Tigresa, and my dog Skipper making feelings of sorrow disappear slowly. I became an expert at blocking reality. I learned to focus on things and patterns. I counted trees to make even numbers. Odd ones frustrated me. I paid close attention to the way a passerby would move his or her feet, created patterns on the old cobblestones of the beaten town and stared at the different shapes the clouds would make as the wind slowly disintegrated them. Days went by with no news of my brothers' whereabouts. Every day that passed,

Mama's cheeks sank from the loss of appetite and the incessant flow of tears. She switched impatiently from the radio to the television and to the newspaper to become aware of any news. The radio did not help, for it played recklessly nerve-fraying songs:

La tumba del	The revolutionary's
guerrillero	tomb,
adonde, adonde,	where, where
adonde esta ,	where could it be,
su madre esta	his mother
preguntando	is asking,
nadie le respondera	no one will answer.

The distressed parents kept close together. Religion kept us strong, as God would be the only one that could be trusted and relied upon. Although we meant no harm, we now needed to watch out for *Orejas*, as they called government officials disguised as civilians who spied for "traitors." An *Oreja* could be anyone, even a blood relative. It was unfortunate how many innocent people died due to calumny and the envious disease of people who wanted to harm others. Rumors spread, later proven true, that one day an *Oreja* walked into a family's home and asked for the virginity of their only daughter. When the father refused, they accused him of being a traitor and he disappeared by "accident—he too ran into a land mine." The news was reported. Such incidents increased by substantial numbers in those days: a landmine encounter, a robbery, a car wreck, the type of mishaps that happen in countries where check and balances are not in place. Two weeks went by without a word of the boys that were taken, but…no battles were reported.

"No news is good news," said a neighbor to Mama.

Then suddenly one day the sounds of death infiltrated our town again. Everyone rushed outside their homes; we saw a hearse slowly approaching down the road, covered partially by a black and red flag. It was the most ominous vehicle I have ever seen: my stomach sunk at the thought of any of my brothers occupying such hair-raising space. People stood still as they saw the hearse slowly approaching, and I could almost hear their hearts beating as they asked themselves who might be inside. The hearse drove by unhurriedly, about five miles per hour, playing a classical tune through its loud speakers. It was music similar to that of a horror movie, which tenses your nerves and rattles your heart. It continued to drive slowly while playing its death tune. It passed by our house without stopping and vanished slowly into the center of the town. Relieved and nearly fainting, Mama sat on her wooden chair, relieved that it was not destined for our house, but saddened for the family where the hearse would make its final stop.

"When will this nightmare be over?" Mama sobbed "One that I wish to be awakened from. No news for weeks and this is how we discover what is really happening."

The town's people followed the hearse to its final destination as it delivered the news to the unfortunate family. It was their only boy and a schoolmate of my brothers. Mama shivered as she prayed for her sons to come home safely to her longing arms. A few days later a boy came to our door announcing, "A letter Doña Nena!" Opening it quickly, Mama thanked God that my brothers were alive and still together! I felt as if I had been through a long-winded race. The way my heart sped up with joy for seeing Mama smile again was a rare event. Retreating to an altar in the corner of the kitchen, she offered the Virgin Mary and Jesus a prayer for each one of us and thanked him repeatedly for allowing her young sons to live.

"We are surviving. Please tell everyone, I love them," the letter concluded.

"Come to the farm!" Papa suggested, but only barely excited, for once there, he had to limit his nightly expeditions. Life was easy for them, compared to mine. They did not need to lure me to the farm. I was ready to go! But one thing our town aimed at, perhaps more than oxygen, was the ability to please our Holy Father and Mother up in the heavens, in the hope that they would bless our existence on earth. Thus, before retreating to the farm once more, we waited until the much-anticipated annual celebration of the virgin

Purisima, one of the most popular celebrations in the country.

"Can your daughter accompany our Mother Mary on the float?" A fervent servant of God asked Mama.

"*Sí*, it's an honor!" Mama agreed with a proud smile.

Ileana as an angel for *La Purisima*

Of course, how could she refuse? After all, my face still resembled that of an untainted angel on Earth. The day of the celebration came, and I was dressed in a silky dress with wings attached to my back. They placed me on top of a tropically decorated float, surrounded by palm leaves and scented fresh flowers. They instructed me to stand still and straight, my hands up in prayer, poised, serious and angelical. I rode alongside Virgin Mary throughout the entire town as people shouted, *"¿Quien causa tanta alegria?* Who causes so much happiness?" And the devout followers replied shouting repeatedly, "The Immaculate Conception of Mary!"

Volunteers who rested at every participating house carried her and me. The procession grew bigger and children waited patiently for the abundant foods and goody bags filled with home-made sugar cane sweetened candy, wooden toys, freshly cut sugar canes, oranges and limes. Every house that took part appeared decorated beauti-fully with palm leaves and personalized altars. Homeowners distributed food and souvenirs to people who prayed, sang and continued *Las Griterias*. Eventually, tired of standing still watching as children, including my own brother Benjamin, indulged in the delectable treats, I stressed out about not receiving my well-deserved portions. I had waited all year for this event, but as the daughter of one of the most active Catholic servants in town, I had to earn my reward. The job of an angel is not easy. As people prayed and cried to the Virgin and me, I found it almost impossible to contain my laughter from their serious and convincing faces, but resumed my posture immedi-ately when the penetrating stare of Mama caught even my slightest smile.

"She was born smiling," someone had said. My heart throbbed again when I noticed that Benjamin and Mama held many goody bags in their hands for me.

"This is special for your angel!" the homeowners told Mama, handing her an even larger bag.

Soon after the famous nine-day *Griterias*, the town's people resumed their normal routine with a much quieter tone; their throats must have been sore from the shouting as they enjoyed serenity. My reward was instant celebrity status and indulgence in traditional candies and sweet sugar cane. During these special celebrations, people became closer, sheltered beneath religious beliefs that brought hope to their hearts, as well as the hospitable social gatherings that kept them civilized. During those nine holy days, the town felt peaceful, and the pain of loss from loved ones and death threats by criminals appeared more endurable. The unity of hearts withstands any evil war craft.

9

Farewell,
Beautiful Socorro

Ileana and Socorro

NO ONE APPRECIATES those we love fully, until it's too late and they're gone, Mama would often say. Besides bombs and bloody killings, the war brought other unexpected gifts. At that time, Cuba came to assist Nicaragua with education and medicine including limbs to replace those that had been lost to the war, and as a result, we had an influx of Cuban doctors and teachers.

Nicaragua went into a state of emergency, the economy crumbled and Cuba came in to our aid, bringing to my sisters' doors a few decent-looking admirers from the neighboring coast of Cuba. Uncle Fidel Castro, as Nicaraguan politicians referred to him, came in to remind Nicaraguans of the positive aspects of communism and therefore sent his supply of free-educated teams of doctors and teachers to increase our literacy rate from what would be about 12% to 50%. Although many women fell in love, married and moved to the island of Cuba, my sisters remained rooted to their home and family. Therefore, after the involuntary draft, my brothers brought home a new war friend and a Nicaraguan. He fought side-by-side with them and became war brothers. He was tall and had broad shoulders, deep dark eyes and black curly hair that made Socorro passionate. Upon his arrival, she dropped her broom, enchanting her suitor with her thin sensual waistline, wavy auburn hair that stretched past her waist and her flirty honey-brown eyes. Chemistry between the two lovebirds was said to be immediate. His visits became more frequent, and my sister began to wonder if they had a future together.

"He is the only good thing war has brought to me," she bragged to her friends.

The academic year in college ended a few months later, and the sign on their car read *"Recién Casados."* At that time, I did not quite understand the meaning of marriage; I simply waited for the much-anticipated reception. On the special day, people came in and out delivering bottles of sodas, food, cake, balloons, tables and chairs. Mama hurried all over the place giving orders, and Socorro spent all day in her room, nervous and restless. As usual, I spent most of the day playing with Benjamin, unaware of what this day would bring into my sister's future. After I had become tired, I went to her room to see her and waited as she diligently brushed her beautiful hair. She allowed me to brush it a couple of times before proceeding to change into her wedding gown. Her dress was simple, and as she turned, the soft satin and the dazzling decorations against her unfurled into a beautiful silhouette.

"I wish to wear a dress like you," I said.

"You will," she said, while she applied make-up to her young face. Intrigued by the whiteness of her dress and the softness of the satin, I asked why her dress could not be pink instead. Kneeling down to my level, she explained, "White represents the purity of a woman; it means that I have never been married before and that I deserve my groom-to-be."

"Deserve him?" I questioned. But the true question that boggled my mind was whether he deserved my beautiful sister.

Holding my light blue dress in her hand, Mama came into the room and became teary when she saw my sister wearing her purity dress. I stood by unnoticed while listening to all the advice Mama gave her, including what to expect on the first wedding night. Baffled as to what was going on, or even what language they were speaking, I quickly changed into the light blue dress and headed out to the patio with my back zipper still open.

"Go sit down," Ernestina ordered. She had volunteered to assist with the wedding. "Your mama will kill me if your dress gets dirty," she scolded while assisting me with my zipper issue.

We headed to the town's cathedral and were awed to see that beyond its gold sculptured walls, pillars and every sculpture of the saints were adorned and fragranced with flowers from the forest, including the orchids that never failed to be present in my life. The holy cathedral was decorated to celebrate and bless the step Socorro was about to take. I sat proudly poised, sang with the church choir and waited for my sister's grand entrance. Suited to their best, my older siblings stepped inside the church, confident as usual. Benjamin followed, smiling and wearing a suit as well. He sat next to me on the white linen chairs, and we waited impatiently for the merrymaking to begin. We were not sure what the whole thing was exactly about, but knew for sure that the party would bring an abundance of decadent treats and a buffet of delectable food. Our waiting felt eternal as we sat there like mummies under the supervision of Ernestina, whose main role that day was to keep us clean, at least until the ceremony concluded. Startled by the sound of the deafening church bell, we jumped out of our seats and took our positions. My oldest sister appeared angelic, ascending from heaven as she walked down the aisle holding onto proud Papa's arm. Seeing her so beautiful and hearing Mama sob caused me to worry. Socorro had cared for me and had served as my second mother when Mama was not around, or whenever she was too busy and too troubled chasing after Papa. Memories rushed through my mind of my sister playing with me and carrying me on her back. Before I knew it, I was laughing uncontrollably. Laugher had become a normal event and a substitute for nervousness. Benjamin hushed me with teary eyes, reminding me that everyone was watching. The priest's sermon felt never-ending; my sister exchanged rings with her groom; Mama and Papa gave my sister to him and I stood there naive as to what was to come next.

"Why are my parents giving away Socorro? Who is going to take care of me now?" I wondered at that moment. More questions intruded into my mind, and I no longer felt hungry. The ceremony ended, and the long-awaited moment that Benjamin and I had been waiting for came. Frenzied by the music, food and the crowd, my brother and I forgot about our sister, at least temporarily. We enjoyed all the things denied in our dietary regimen and joyfully rotted our teeth with decadent desserts and a variety of soft drinks and fruit punches. After feasting, we made fools of ourselves, dancing and running around until we became dizzy and had to catch a breath of fresh air. Then outside by the patio we spotted our parents hugging my sister next to a car decorated with streaming crepe paper and colorful balloons.

"I will miss you, *mi niña,*" Mama cried. I ran to my sister, crying and clinging to her dress and I begged her not to leave me. "Why are you leaving?"

"*¡Vóz no entendes!*" she said.

"You are right. I don't understand."

Suddenly, all of the food came rushing back up through my esophagus, almost forcing me to vomit on my beautiful sister's dress. My heart ached and my mind wondered how I could live without her. Angry at her husband, I stomped on his foot and ran away shouting, "I hate you." Soon after she left, guests danced for a long time to the sounds of rhythmic *cumbias,* boleros and body magnetizing classical romantics and eventually retreated to their homes upon the first rays of the morning light. Our house felt empty. For the first time, I felt an indescribable loneliness in my heart. I retreated to Socorro's room, looked inside her empty closet and lay on her bed. I fell asleep comforted by her still scented pillow for the first time; I awoke to a smaller family. The next morning, resuming her routine in the kitchen, Mama made *Gallo Pinto* for breakfast. She chopped the weeping onions into tiny pieces blaming them for her tears as she married black refried beans with the soft steamed white rice grains, stirring them into the hot oil until the meal became one. My brothers were up early and pestered my sister Francisca to wake up. Silence was prominent as we sat at our long table staring at the one empty chair. We could not contain our tears. The feeling of loss felt heavy, and the uncertainty of her future as being married to a soldier, made us all feel uneasy and desolated.

"La vida sigue," Mama counseled, reminding us that life goes on.

"It's the cycle of life that some come and go," Papa added.

We were silent. My parents' remarks sounded convincing, but at that moment it did not seem to sink in.

10

Once Upon a Lost Love

Juan Carlos at the farm.

ALMOST A YEAR had passed since Socorro married. My sister Francisca came home from college again, along with my brothers Ramón and

Francisco. Socorro would spend her first Christmas away from home in the company of her new family. She promised to visit for the New Year if she did not end up in Cuba for a free education like many of her friends. Mama's favorite recipe, *Gallina Rellena*, required the killing of a farm chicken, so Mama prepared for the task by whistling. The yearly assassination of the lucky hen boiled my blood as Mama went outside and proceeded to twist the hen's neck until it broke and the chicken stopped kicking. Used to the way of life, Mama came in a bit annoyed with me and placed the chicken in a large boiling pot of water until the feathers were loose enough to be extracted from the skin.

"You're committing a crime!" I accused.

No matter how hard she attempted to explain the food chain to me, I still had a difficult time assimilating a chicken's death. Christmas had a peculiar charm for my brother's spirit though. Juan Carlos, the fifth child, was one of those surreal characters that managed to bring magic into life.

"He has an enlarged heart," the family doctor reminded every time Mama worried about his latest abrupt mood swings and sorrowful regrets.

"Ho! Ho! Ho!" announced my golden-hearted brother when he walked into the house dressed as Santa Claus as he had done for the past few years. While tumbling and tripping on each other, Benjamin and I ran to greet and snatch his large bag. He smiled and ran away from us, all the while teasing that he was not going to give us anything. Lacking enough air in our lungs to catch him, we waited patiently until Santa decided to give in.

"Not too bad for a big-bellied guy, eh?" he bragged, "Not bad at all."

Seeing my brother full of life was like seeing a magnificent stallion horse, one that runs a wild spirit, but the type that if ever tamed could be your best friend and companion. Juan Carlos was the type of young man who would give it all for a good cause, love most of all. Perhaps it is the law of life that the good suffer on earth and the wicked suffer in hell, but regardless, it is hard to bear the suffering of those we love the most. My handsome brother, wonderful, full of life and with dreams, was yet to be tested under this law. The life of a remarkable young man, who won most of the ribbon races in town and inspired many girls to dream about him, took a tragic turn. Soon after his first military assignment, he would soon realize that vulnerability and pain could come at any time. Although he never told his own story to us kids, I heard the story from family members when I questioned his uncivilized drinking habits and temper tantrums. Of course, adults related the story in a flat manner, without the grace and imagination of a child. Listening attentively, I recreated a romantic but catastrophic love story of my own, and through my imagination, drifted deep into the cloud forest where the nightmare was said to have taken place.

168

I began to journey as I heard the tale of two young and brave sweethearts. At seventeen years of age, Juan Carlos had joined the military by draft. Trained only for a few days, he went to battle where he met the beautiful and young Esmeralda. Those who knew her said that she was like a beautiful horse, lean and with a wild spirit like his, with the eyes of a tigress and the glowing skin of a panther. She was to be his twin soul; the one that sparked his fire and made his heart beat hundreds of miles per hour, the one who astounded him and gave him butterflies in his stomach. My imagination wandered along the trails my brother and Esmeralda followed that day. It was a rainy afternoon deep in the forest, far away from home, far away from reality. Though it was soggy and muddy, Juan Carlos marched along the forest in perfect harmony and steady alertness. Close behind followed Esmeralda. Clearing the way, Timoteo, his combat comrade, cut through the thick trees using a sharp machete. With hearts hammering at every strange noise, they moved ahead cautiously until they found ground zero. It was said that, defeated by exhaustion, some of the soldiers fell asleep, while others took turns standing guard. Esmeralda rested gently as Juan Carlos held her in his arms. She kissed him goodnight and assured him of her love for him. They slept peacefully until it was time to resume their walk.

"Wake up soldier," the captain urged, poking Juan Carlos's boot with his rifle and moving steady from one soldier to the next.

It was a glowing morning, and the sunlight filtered through the trees illuminating every step. The smell of moist leaves reminded them of home. The sound of the wild brought memories of peace, and a rainbow over the horizon signaled hope. Then Juan Carlos's sweet 17-year-old smile would be wiped from his face by the unbearable sounds that would resonate in his ears and heart forever.

"GET DOWN!" soldiers yelled.

They were under attack. However, disobeying the law of combat, Juan Carlos grabbed Esmeralda and pulled her to his side. Frightened by the sounds of war and blood that was tainting the forest red, they held onto each other as he shot at whoever came their way.

"I love you, Esmeralda. I will marry you after this is over," he promised. Esmeralda clung to him like a child clings onto his mother. Time went by when they realized most soldiers were gone. Loud thunder resonated through the leaves as the overcast sky warned an indolent storm. The battle had finally ended, leaving a stained forest behind. Frightened and in shock by the petrifying silence, Esmeralda left his side attempting to run away. Before he could stop her, bullets shot by a wounded opposition soldier with an AK47 persuaded her to remain there forever.

"No!" Juan Carlos cried. The seventeen-year-old boy had become a man.

Shooting violently until the soldier no longer moved, Juan Carlos emptied his rifle for the first time. His one true love ended as he hugged Esmeralda and her blood warmed his cold body. The weapon that stole her life had split her body in half right before his eyes. Esmeralda had joined the service in the hopes of exciting adventures as described by revolutionary women enthusiasts. Silence blocked his ears as he sat there in despair until his compatriots forced him to flee. My dear brother received a gift of war he did not wish to accept. Retreating, as ordered by the General, he and his fellow fighters ran out of the wilderness without stopping. In his clouded and delirious state, he managed to ask other soldiers he came into contact if they had seen any of his two older brothers. But at their negative nods, he simply lost hope of seeing them again.

"Your brother Ramon, the tall and skinny one, was seen last carrying only a machete because he had been sanctioned," a soldier from another battalion informed him. Juan Carlos was convinced that he had to be dead. He then described our brother with the long hair. "Have you seen my brother Francisco?" he asked everywhere.

"No," a soldier would shake his head, "I'm sorry."

Hopeless, wet and cut off from his feelings, he kept walking toward the direction he only knew—

back home into the shelter of the cloud forest. Mama followed Papa's recommendations to go to the farm. She waited anxiously there for news of her boys until the day when the dogs barked at the sight of a shadow looming over the hills.

"Go away," Papa instructed the intruder, aiming his gun, only to lower it when he saw Juan Carlos emerging from the forest. Nearly lifeless, my brother approached the house and soon fainted after crossing the threshold of the house. For days he ran an unusually high fever that caused him terrible nightmares. In his delirium, he would shout, "Death! Esmeralda!"

The thought of not seeing her other two sons broke Mama's heart again, but Ramon arrived a few days later with a story similar to that of Carlos on his lips. A week later Francisco came as well, numb from the traumas of a futile war. Benjamin and I were still oblivious to the pain my family was experiencing. Life hadn't changed for us. We continued fighting over our toys and waiting anxiously for the next holiday to come so that we could open up our gifts. Therefore, submerged deeply into my own childhood paradise, I asked Mama how many more days there were before Christmas.

"Too many to count," she responded.

Christmas did come again; however, this time we waited all night for our memorable Santa, who never arrived. Saddened and disappointed, we woke up and ran to his room.

"Why didn't you come last night?" We asked Juan Carlos, poking him on his head. He yelled at us, and we ran away crying to Mama because he threatened to hit us if we bothered him again.

"What is wrong with him?"

"He has grown up, and he is too old to play Santa tricks," Mama calmly explained.

"Then can someone else be Santa?"

Smiling, Mama nodded and walked away, and we went on about our business, playing, eating and fighting, oblivious of our brother's suffering from hardships and sorrows. He came later, and sat next to us while we played war with Benjamin's plastic soldiers. Removing them away abruptly, he apologized for his earlier behavior and gave us a strong hug. We still felt grief that he hadn't been Santa, but we returned his hug anyway. After tickling us, he went into town and we were left playing in the yard. Life had killed his spirit. From that point on, he was a dead man walking with no dreams—a living carcass without hope and love in his heart. Bringing more sorrow to my already troubled Mama, he would come home claiming to see "blue demons," as people called it when drunkards were heavily intoxicated and haunted by wild hallucinations.

"Help!" Mama yelled one night when Juan Carlos came home intoxicated, screaming and threatening that he was going to kill himself and everyone around him. And Mama ran quickly to hide whatever weapons might have been at hand.

The neighbors came quickly to our rescue and helped to hold him down on his bed. Mama pleaded for the men to tie him up to the bed until he finally fell asleep. The next morning, he woke up with a massive headache and bruises on his arms left by the ropes that had kept him alive. My new angry brother walked past me without a word.

"He had a nightmare," Mama tried to explain.

A nightmare indeed, one too horrific to be true, but true nonetheless. This was another tragic product of war. It transformed my lovely brother into one I no longer knew, a man haunted forever by feverish nightmares and mood swings. It created an uncertain destiny edged in stone. Then three years later, as Juan Carlos prepared to go to college, he became an involuntary, but proud Papa. After dating a woman that refused to stop pursuing him, and for which he was ten years her junior, he came upon a sudden surprise and faced the challenge of becoming a responsible Papa. And upon the continuous harassment to become a soldier again to pursue a senseless war, and after he had been in a car accident when his military jeep overturned and was also later pushed against an oncoming car by his own girlfriend, he was left nearly paralyzed physically and mentally. Perhaps, he should have gone to heaven that day.

"!Dios mio!" Mama cried rushing outside after hearing a loud noise of a crash right across from our home.

"His fiancé, Maria Magdalena, pushed him to the road!" the neighbors told Mama.

"They seemed to argue and so she pushed him off onto the oncoming traffic," witnesses recounted in disbelief.

Crying hysterically, Mama nearly disappeared with grief at the sight of Carlo's jugular pulsing. It was a miracle that it remained intact. The impact of his body against the vehicle tore his clothes and his body became swollen and bloody. For sure, she thought he was gone, but I was convinced that my brother might have had nine lives; after all, he had come home from war, hadn't he? Moreover, he did survive that time again for he was a fighter. A few months later, after he physically recovered, he left to a place people called "the land of the brave and the free." He boarded a public bus from *La Estación* and left his family behind, equipped only with a backpack and hopes for a better future, or at the very least, a more peaceful one.

Waving goodbye, I shed more tears, wondering when, if ever, things might be the same again. Santa never returned to visit our home. Slowly but surely, family dinners became smaller. The rambunctious house that once accommodated so many comfortably now felt bigger, quieter and lonelier. Pursuing their dreams of graduating from college, Francisca, Francisco and Ramon moved to the capital city of Managua for good, four hours away from our town. Mama worried about leaving them in other people's homes. Therefore, she begged

Papa to take her to Managua to visit, as she could not detach herself emotionally from them. I jumped in the back of the car as it drove up the winding road. I felt excited to see my brothers and sister again. I entertained myself by counting the trees by the roadside. Obsessed in creating even pairs of all the things I saw by the road, I counted nearly everything I saw until my stomach felt upset and I earned a headache of intolerable magnitude.

"Stop the car!" I urged.

Papa pulled over by the nearest fruit stand. I emptied my stomach, but the headache crippled me for the rest of the way. Arriving later at Managua didn't make things better. After that dreadful drive, my clothes were drenched by the humidity. The convolution of traffic exhausted me. Vehicles rushed from all directions. Overwhelmed, we circled around the town; we drove into a jungle, one that appeared harsher and dangerous. Uncomfortable from the overwhelming heat, Mama rerouted her thoughts of reuniting with her children, and this gave her the strength to endure it. We took turns visiting each of the houses my siblings lived in during that time. We saw Ramon first, who had lost significant weight, loved the busy life but was distraught from getting a less than perfect grade on his test. Then we traveled to see Francisco who despite his war traumas and random outbreaks acquired the reputation of an honorable engineer in the making. Both of my brothers still allowed themselves to dream.

176

"We are going to the fair!" they announced, surprising me.

"What's a fair?" I asked.

"You'll see!" In the past, Francisco had taken the place of Papa when he was not around and pleasing us would still be rewarding to him. I entered the fair that was lit by electricity instead of fireflies, wanting to acquire everything in sight. I ignored my pounding headache. I rode the wondrous Ferris wheel and for a few moments indulged in one of the small pleasures of life.

"!Algodón!" called a cotton candy vendor.

Reaching into his pocket, Ramon took out the only córdoba he had left and then handed Benjamin and me an unbelievably gigantic cotton candy held on a bamboo stick. Mama nodded that it was okay for us to eat it, allowing us the pleasure of sugar on this special day. Laughing at the sight of the treat spreading all over my face, we resembled the image of a happy family once again. A few moments later, I was attacked by a cough, my face reddened, and I couldn't breathe. Tightly squeezing my stomach and pounding me on my back, Papa hit me so that I would expel the string of bamboo that had caught in my throat. I was unable to speak well for a long time; my sore throat made it almost impossible to swallow.

"On the bright side, Ileana is going to take a break from talking!" Francisca told everyone, and all laughed in agreement. The next day we prepared to go back to our small confinement. Giving her

177

blessings to my brothers, Mama prayed to God to shelter them under his holy embrace. Leaving her children behind as we headed back home, Mama wiped her tears and waved goodbye. I was glad to leave the commotion of the city and to return to my quiet town. Although I missed my brothers and sisters terribly, nothing compared to the blessings of my ordinary life.

11

The Toll of the Hour

I CAN'T HELP but feel a certain chill at the toll of the hour, the tick of the minutes and the tock of the seconds passing by. No doubt, it is the immense power of innocence that shelters a child's world as he or she wanders through it, oblivious to the events that take place.

Our lives were changing. Nothing remained the same for anyone. Confused and unable to make sense of what was going on with my loved ones, I turned once more to nature for relief. We were not the only ones affected by war and other unforeseen calamities. It saddened me deeply to see the forest of my dreams vanish before my eyes by the steady deforestation and the fires caused by the unrelenting weaponry. From one mountain to the next, enemy troops battled without compassion until done for that day. When fires weren't threatening, greed and temptation for highly-desired wood desecrated my forest. The rich landscape began to scar along with my family, and I felt more and more vulnerable with each toll of the church's old clock announcing the hour to the sound of Für Elise. And as the bewitching of the song played throughout the town intoxicated my blood, I could not detach from the irony of its lyrical similarities to the war, its ups and downs and the apparent lyrics of happiness, despair and whimsical heroism. I wondered often if the war would stop like the song, leaving only distant memories behind. Would we return to our enchanting beginnings? I had learned about the lyrical miracles of the song through the teachings of our family priest and through the obsessive replays in my mother's record player. I didn't learn the title to these bewitching lyrics until later in life, but Für Elise followed me throughout my childhood through the shattering of bullets whistling on rooftops and the echoes of explosions.

Depending solely upon a hint of luck and a miracle of God, the Nicaraguans' destiny became indefinitely unclear. Returning to the farm to escape from the endless years of war, and not for vacation, Papa worried over caring for his loved ones, while abiding as a good citizen. More often, uninvited guests with machine-guns slung over their shoulders appeared at the farm and demanded services. At that point, it did not matter which side you were with, if any; their weapons made you quickly decide. One day, the dogs' persistent bark alerted us that some of these guests were about to arrive. Papa alerted us to come inside the house. Suddenly, armed and hungry soldiers rushed into our house and helped themselves to whatever they could find. Papa remained calm and collective. He provided the food they demanded with the hope that they would leave before the opposition also decided to stop by.

"Come here, sweetie," the captain instructed me, patting on his lap.

Papa swallowed heavily and if one knew him well, one would know he felt nervous. I did as the soldier instructed me to do and as my father had trained me to behave, especially during particular times where the life of others depended on me. I sat on his lap appearing emotionless after Dad gave me a nod in agreement. I remember the soldier's eyes and they reminded me of a jaguar. They were green, the color of my forest, but also red. Perhaps, he had seen much bloodshed, and his eyes had photographed the images. His hair was covered with a bandana. Then wrapping his arms around me, he asked my name. He also smelled like sulfur, which gave me instant chills, "Ileana" I replied, disgusted by the smell of his weaponry. I realized then that they were carrying the devil with their evil and sulfuring weapons.

"Which side are you with?" I then dared to ask.

He stared at me deeply and ignoring my question, he asked me another question, "Are there other people in the house, sweetie?"

"No," I replied while returning his stare. I learned to control my emotions by holding my breath a bit. It helped to slow my heartbeat as well. He then pushed me off him. "Go on and play!" he said, and then turned to Papa, "Your daughter will very soon become a woman. Take reasonable care of her."

Nodding in agreement, Papa moved to the side as the soldier helped himself to more food. Once they were gone, my family gathered again, and I saw the stress of our new way of life etched on everyone's tense faces.

"Good job, Ileana. Next time, don't ask any questions," Papa told me.

The next morning, Papa tried to resume a normal schedule. He invited me to see a reservoir built to pump water. This was only a convenience to Papa, since rainfall was plentiful and we didn't need to store any water as a reserve.

"Ileana, come!" he invited.

"Si Papa!" I gladly replied, jumping up and down with joy.

"Then go and ask Mama."

"Mama! May I go with Papa to the water reservoir?"

"No, remember the last time when you almost drowned crossing the river?" she reminded me.

"Please, Mama, please!" I insisted, "I'll be safe with Papa."

"Do as you please, but don't return crying."

Shrugging her shoulders, she resumed her heavenly job and continued to pray by the fire. I climbed up on Papa's saddle, without reservations, and he wrapped his arms around me. It was raining as usual, and I could hear the unsynchronized raindrops fall on leaves. I was certain the rain would serve to appease the turbulence of the country and would clear all bloodshed from battlefields and broken paths. Papa enjoyed the land, and I enjoyed his company; it made me feel valuable. On our way, Papa pointed to the different types of moss, the fallen trees and Mama's favorite ferns. As we went further into the forest, the fog became denser and menacing. Soon the horse stopped and refused to cross the river. I wished just then to have been praying with Mama instead, but it was too late. Papa poked the horse with his spurs and forced the hesitant animal into the angry river as the animal twisted his neck in rebellion. The strength of the river would be fearsome for anyone else except for my brave Papa who continued to poke our mount with his spurs. Flashbacks of our last visit came to mind, and I cried again.

"Oh no, not again," he reproached. "You must stop this silliness. Nothing happens with water unless you fear it. I will help you lose this fear once and for all."

"Please, don't!" I continued to cry.

Papa rode for what appeared an endless period of time, with a quiet and stern tone. He simply ignored my cries and pleas. We arrived at the intimidating water reservoir. He got off his horse, pulled me down and sat me on a nearby tree trunk. Loneliness stroked at my organs as I sat in the dark forest, wet and isolated, in the company of a robot-like father whose lack of fear was fearful enough to make me perspire, even on a cool and rainy day. After careful inspection of the reservoir and after taking measurements, Papa looked back at me, smiled and said we were done. I took a deep breath in relief; it felt as if life was returning to my frightful body. But before I sang in victory, Papa picked me up by my underarms, and instead of landing on the horse I ended up on the edge of that deep and dark reservoir. Sobbing, I begged Papa not to leave me there.

"Go on," he demanded firmly, "Cross!"

Looking down at the deep water, I couldn't control how much my body was shaking. My cries probably became louder as Papa became more persistent.

"Don't look at the water," he demanded.

"That's easy for you to say," I said.

"Very well, I guess your Mama will have to come get you."

He began to walk away towards his horse. At the thought of being left there alone, I began to move my trembling legs, but my fear and uncontrollable shrieking made it nearly impossible to stand upright. Crossing a rectangular 20-foot water reservoir wouldn't be funny to anyone in her right mind. Crying and tremulous, I tried walking straight and fast on the narrow borders of that deep and unfriendly reservoir. Halfway across, I froze. Papa threatened me with his stern look. "Finish or you will stay here." At that point, I wasn't sure of what scared me the most, Papa or the dark reservoir. My stomach sank, my hands felt sweaty, and my whole body felt numb from my shallow breathing. I could no longer feel my face. The fallen leaves dazzled me as I looked into the water. Hypnotized, I found myself wanting to jump in instead. But before I lost my mind entirely, Papa pulled me toward him, and I stared straight back into his penetrating hazel eyes.

"What's with you?" he asked annoyed, placing me back onto the horse while shaking his head. "There's no room for fear in this world. Eventually, you'll have to face your fears. Life is not all games and dreams," he continued as he guided his horse to speed up.

At that point, I had nothing to say. Perhaps I would have understood if he had leveled down to me and spoke in tongues appropriate to my age. On the way back home, the clip-clop of the horses' hooves and the remnants of the raindrops were all that I could hear. Their sound on the muddy puddles penetrated my ears; I felt miserable and guilty for letting Papa down. Then again, my ears clogged with Papa's continuous and grave rhetoric on how and why I should lose my fear of water. To him water was man's best friend.

"Look around you," he would say. "Without water, this beautiful landscape wouldn't be here and neither would we!"

At that time, I could not tell whether water was a close friend or not; to me, it had a short temper and did not like to be abused for its affability. Papa and I were similar in many ways, but the one thing that I could not match him at was my ownership of fear and his lack of it. After all, who was I to blame him for what he'd just done to me? Parents always want the best for their children, although the best isn't always what it appears to be. Back in the safety of my beloved cabin, we were welcomed with a hot cup of cacao drink and sugar-sweetened beans wrapped in freshly-made corn tortillas. The aroma of Mama's food brought life back to me. Hugging her strongly, I told her that I loved her. She looked into my eyes gently and said, "I can tell by your face that you have been through a storm of your own, haven't you?" Unable to reply, I simply hugged her again. She sat me on her lap and gave Papa a piece of her subtle mind.

"You did it again?" Mama reproached.

"Yes, I did and will do it again as long as it is necessary," he said proudly. "She needs to learn to face her fears."

"That is not the way to make her unafraid! All you are doing is making things worse for her and for you!"

Saddened as usual by him, Mama sat next to me while I played with my food. After eating, the heavy storm hit again and temporarily distracted me. Lightning was striking more frequently, and the sky had turned darker. Raindrop after raindrop, the rain slowly filled the riverbanks. Hour after hour, every heavenly drop helped to create a powerful stream that slithered down the hills with a hypnotizing strength, capable of taking on whatever crossed its path. I rested by the windowsill and watched the steady downpour of the rain alone.

"Ileana! Keep away from the window! You know it is not good to stand by a window when there is lightning," Mama called out to me, interrupting my enchantment. Eventually, Benjamin joined me and pointed out the powerful mountain stream that had turned into a river and was beginning to flood the plantations. That evening Benjamin shared his plastic soldier toys with me as we harmoniously played out a battle using the sound effects of the storm.

Back in the kitchen, Mama stood by the fire whistling and cooking at the same time. Her spirit ran high. She appeared to have applied make-up on her face. Her hair was brushed more than once, something Mama would usually do for particular outings. She busied herself again by making *buñuelos* for Papa to enjoy with a cup of coffee upon his return. Regardless of whether Mama and Papa argued, her role, as a homemaker remained the same. Somehow, Mama found peace in her prayers and cooking. Making *buñuelos* became a routine as she slowly rolled the corn dough over and over, stretching every ball into a small one. Once she had rolled over thirty small balls, she went on to make sugar cane syrup to top them.

"Want to help?" she asked. "You mix some brown sugar, some cinnamon and some vanilla, and there you have it. Help me spread it over the buñuelos." She handed me the syrup. I accepted, relieved to be back with her.

"Can I sprinkle sugar on top?"

"Sure! Just don't eat any yet."

Annoyed by not being able to put some of the sugar topping in my mouth, I turned to look at our remaining new guard dog, which was hiding under the table.

"What is wrong with Misuterri?" I asked.

"He's been hiding there since the storm began. He's scared of lightning, remember?" Mama said laughing.

According to Mama, Misuterri was near a tree one day when lightning hit him and as a result, had since been scared of storms. How funny, I thought. Our tough guard dog was now a scared little puppy under the table. I couldn't help but sympathize with him. After all, I knew better than anybody how it felt to be afraid of something. Therefore, after eating some *buñuelos*, I joined him under the table. His puppy eyes, which were teary, touched my heart. I held him in my arms and felt his heart beating fast. Rubbing his back and listening to Mama's prayers and the crackling of the burning wood was the perfect recipe for putting us both to sleep. The rain kept pouring; Papa finally came home soaked from the heavenly showers and enjoyed the warm buñuelos and his favorite drink, a strong black cup of coffee served in a clay jug. My parents sat by the fire and conversed as if nothing had ever happened. I later found myself in my cozy bed.

I slept through the night until the restless cock woke me up to another beautiful morning. By then the rain had ceased, leaving behind a colorful rainbow and the tantalizing smell of wet soil and refreshing mist. Slipping on my red water boots, I headed outside to watch the herding of the cows, as I knew that was going to be the main job of the day. Routing the cows to the right, Papa looked at me and called for me to join him. It didn't take long for his charm to cast a magic charm on me again. After all, he was my hero and the best Papa in the world. I knew that deep inside his heart, I was still his baby girl. So there we went again, seeking the next tough challenge.

Mornings at the farm were always engulfing and eventful. The mountains dominated the landscape and the mist circling the sky released cool morning dew—a commodity to my lungs. Wearing blue jeans and my red water boots, I stood outside, stretching my arms up in the air as I took in deep breaths. Absorbing every second in the isolation I'd desired for so long while we were in the City of Mists, I hoped that life would stand still and let me stay in that moment forever. Oxygen released by the variety of trees and plants, including all of the exotic orchids, brought unforgettable joy to my heart. Although striking and at times mystical, our forest farm was also full of routines and daily adventures, involving every person and animal. Everyone had a job to do and a contribution to make. Cows grazed and gave quality milk, the bulls rested on top of the cows, chickens lay and guarded their eggs, snakes slithered and stole chicken eggs, and workers assumed their positions. I had the most difficult task of touring my own farm and supervising the well-being of its wildlife. Papa gestured for me to come quickly as he had already started his work. He knew I was always ready.

Holding Papa's firm hand, I quickly had to face another fear. The challenge was to cross from one side of the corral to the other, between the sharp-horned cows. My head barely reached the udder of a cow, and it wasn't long before I was terrified again. Fearless Papa encouraged me to cross. I managed to cross the stone corral with much more dignity than I had at the reservoir. I then headed inside the dairy barn with renewed spirit to watch the milking process. Singing to the cows while milking them, Pedro, a strong and dedicated worker at the farm signaled for me to try my hand. Pedro was a man whose muscular build gave evidence of his hours of wrestling matches, taming horses and, if required, lifting children. Always laughing and exposing a few missing teeth due to local physical altercations, he went through life without any worries. I stood behind him fascinated.

"Do you want to try it?" he asked.

I sat down on his wooden stool, bent my knees and then carefully massaged the cow's udder, filling up my cup with warm, foamy milk. When done, I walked slowly to the dairy house, trying not to spill, and sat at the kitchen table waiting for Felicia to feed me *Gallo Pinto* and over-easy eggs.

"I don't understand how you can eat so much, child," Felicia would often say in dismay as I drank my large cup of milk and left the dish sparkling clean.

Another day came, and I did what I did best: driving Mama out of her mind. I sang to St. Ysidro, the saint of rain repeatedly while sitting by the window, watching the torrential rain fill the aqueducts again.

San Isidro Labrador	Saint Ysidro take
quita la lluvia	away the rain and
y pon el sol	bring out the sun

Hoping that St. Ysidro would perform the miracle of taking away the rain, I kept singing, but he never listened. The rain continued to pour for several days. My young mind must have forgotten that the green of the rain forest that I loved so much came from such torrential waters as these. Therefore, San Ysidro knew better than granting the wishes of an ignorant child. Water, the very source of life at times, felt as though it would be the end of my life. On stormy days, Mama stayed inside praying many rosaries and novenas. After making the sign of the cross, she would pray to all the saints in heaven for every need: St. Ysidro for the rain, St. Barbara for thunder and lightning, St. Francis de Assisi to protect our animals, and ultimately my sweet sister Amanda, our guardian angel in heaven, for her to intervene on our behalf.

Fearless Papa went about his business as usual, rain or shine. After deluges like this, he would set out to release water from the reservoir. Filling it up excessively wasn't a preventive measure for drought, but rather a way to make it easier to bring water to our farm; therefore, consistent monitoring was needed. After her prayers, Mama laughed with sad sarcasm, "Sure that liar is always checking the reservoir," she would think aloud as she immediately attempted to reword her thoughts.

"Liar…that reservoir that fills up."

"What do you mean, Mama?" I asked. "When is Papa coming home?"

"Never, if he ran into *La Següa*," she said laughing.

I began to worry. "Who is *La Següa?*"

"Come sit right here" she said, and the storytelling began.

"La Següa is a woman who became pregnant by a god. She was a ghastly mother because she abandoned her child to meet her lover one night. The child died, and the god cursed her. She appears

beautiful at first sight, but when approached by a man, she turns into an abomination, one too ugly for a person to look at. She is a witch who lives in the woods but can appear anywhere. She attracts men by walking naked, but as soon as a man touches her, her young and slim body transforms into a corpse. She drives men insane by uttering horrible curses and crying over the lost child she had left to die deep inside the woods," Mama said. Horrified, I wondered if *La Següa* could truly get a hold of Papa.

"Enough of *La Següa,*" Mama concluded. "Let's go and see the pig's feeding instead."

We went outside and became distracted by the feeding frenzy I noticed that a piglet was not eating well and pointed him out to Mama.

"If he doesn't eat, he'll die," she said. I ran to the kitchen, grabbed an old milk bottle, filled it and returned to the spotted piglet.

"Don't, you are altering the cycle of life," Mama warned me.

"I'm not going to let it die," I said.

"Oh, Ileana, when will you stop giving me such headaches?" Mama was still complaining upon Papa's return. Mama told him how I fed the pig with a bottle. Of course, a farmer is never supposed to become attached to his personal food chain, and he admonished me for trying to help the little pig.

"Please let me have it; I'll take care of him," I begged.

"Enough, you can't possibly own every animal in my farm," he refused, annoyed with me as much as Mama was. Papa took advantage of any moment when I professed my concern about an animal to give me a piece of his mind about how a farmer's daughter ought to behave.

"It doesn't make sense for you to try to domesticate every single animal that comes your way. At this rate, you will make me a poor man. God gave us animals, herbs and vegetables for us to eat. It is part of nature, and you have to accept it."

His fatherly advice would go in through one ear and out the other. I was convinced that protecting animals from pain would be one of my many missions. I tried relentlessly to prevent the slaughter of any more animals and, as a result, my parents attempted to hide it from me whenever they needed to "doctor" an animal. Not easily fooled, I was well aware of what doctoring meant, and although I was not successful at preventing future medical catastrophes, at least I made sure they heard my thoughts about the matter; something they truly hated.

"I love you," Mama would always say, "and God loves me, too, because he gives me all the patience in the world to deal with you." But laughing and sticking his tongue out, Benjamin made fun of me, as I did not get my way all the time. In that episode of our lives, we were enjoying absolute innocence.

12

Goose, Be Gone

THEN CAME the goose. As always, there are things we dislike and often wish to discard from of our lives. The beautiful but short-tempered white geese were the ones that kept me on the run daily at the farm. Chasing me around, annoyed by my intrusion, they always tried to bite my behind. Although they often ran away from Papa, they chased me instead, and for this, I hated them deeply. Benjamin and I had a fabulous time playing in the water puddles left by the rain and looking at the rainbow that appeared to touch the mountains in the last of the true light left in the day. Meanwhile, one stubborn goose kept chasing after me. She failed since I was a faster runner, but there were too many narrow escapes.

"Help," I cried out, "This goose is about to get me!"

"Come inside then," Papa urged me while chasing the goose away.

Mama was preparing fresh tortillas and boiled black beans for dinner. Benjamin said he wanted to play with his plastic soldiers and followed Papa back inside the house. The dogs sat lazily out on the porch, and I knew Papa had gone back to work on sharpening his knives and machetes. He always inspected every tool meticulously as he prepared for the next day. I also knew that he would go into his bedroom and ready his clothes in order, while telling Benjamin, "Always be ready to run because a man should never be caught in his underwear, and he should never be caught off guard." He would continue to offer his words of wisdom to his son, but my brother only listened while proceeding with his play. I had often wondered what Papa meant, but just in case, I also left my things ready every evening. It became a handy habit when waking up in the morning and catching up with Papa to round up the cows. I wondered sometimes if God had made a mistake and switched my brother and me before birth. My brother should have been the one chasing after him, and I should have been the one sleeping in late. But God never makes a mistake; we all have our own destiny. Papa stepped out on the porch again.

"It's getting late. Come in now," Papa ordered.

"I'm coming, Papa!" I replied, running away from the goose yet again.

Suddenly, there was an astounding sound, so loud that it left me temporarily deaf. In a matter of seconds, I flew to Papa, who quickly pulled me inside the house, and then flung me to the floor. We were in the line of fire. Enemies had crossed our path again, except this time they had no regard for our meaningless civilian lives. Just a few yards away from where I was just playing, a bomb exploded. We lay on the floor as a rain of bullets perforated our house and more bombs fell to the ground. Papa made us bite onto a cloth rope to prevent us from biting our tongues. We lay as flat as we could, trembling, waiting for our lives to end. Mama prayed to God, to Amanda and to all the saints that came to her mind, making that moment feel more frightful. Benjamin and I trembled with panic. Papa attempted to remain strong as he helplessly held us both in his arms. Fear took possession of our bodies, and after a while, we no longer felt anything. Then a calm feeling of expectancy came over me, and I simply waited to transport into the next life. After all, we were sure to go to heaven for we had prayed enough. We were ready. Our bodies lay still; we held hands and closed our eyes. I felt numb again just as I had felt when I was at the water reservoir, but at one point I was certain I no longer felt any fear. Bullets echoed through the metal roof and the wooden planks on the walls as parts of the house splintered open. It felt endless. Surely, it was a day we could never forget, but it was not the day for us to die. After the attack, we cautiously peeked outside. A nearby bomb had obliterated the goose. Immense guilt over wishing for the goose to stop chasing me and be gone rushed through my body and gave me an uncontrollable chill. If only I could turn back time, and undo my evil thoughts! Tears poured down my chin, and I explained to Mama that everything had been my fault.

"Nothing happens without God's will," she reminded me again and proceeded to clean up the place with no apparent regard for the goose.

"But you don't understand," I insisted, "The goose is gone!"

It was then that she kneeled before me and explained that it was perhaps because of that goose that I was still standing before her. My family agreed to give whatever was left of the goose, a quick but proper burial in order to ease my nerves. From that moment on, I pledged that I would never again wish terrible things on anyone or anything. It was as the saying goes, "No one knows what they have until they lose it." Later, the new geese still chased me, but never as fiercely as the old one. Life on the farm resumed as usual. However, we were skeptical to go out and play and some nights we woke up screaming in cold sweat. Therefore, after endless discussions, Papa and Mama decided that it was time to send my brother away, far away from his homeland where bullets could not touch him and threats of the mandatory draft would not reach him and turn him into a boy soldier.

"Benjamin will go with Juan Carlos," Mama decided one day.

Upon returning to town, Mama pulled me to her arms and hugged me so tightly that I could not breathe.

"What is wrong, Mama?" I asked.

She slowly placed me on her lap and explained to me that my brother Benjamin would soon be leaving to join Juan Carlos in the land of dreams and freedom. I was shocked because even though Benjamin and I had a love-angry relationship as common rivalries between siblings exist, I could not see life without him. He was the only person I played with and the last sibling remaining close to me. Emptiness and desperation filled me as Mama packed his clothes. My brother was just a child, and I could see worry in his large brown eyes as he prepared for a precarious voyage to an unfamiliar land, strange people and unknown adventures. He had never been away from home and Mama. How could he possibly survive at barely eleven years old? To support Mama, I locked my tears away and stopped asking questions. Finally, when I could no longer hold the beast clawing at me, I hid behind the rose bushes in the backyard to cry. I cried for so long that I must have fallen asleep because when I woke up I was on my bed and experiencing another nightmare. When I woke up, I ran to look for my brother.

"Ya se fueron!" Tatiana said.

"What do you mean?" I asked, "They did not take me to say goodbye to him?"

I ran back to my room where I could freely release my tears but had no more left. Despair held me prisoner in my own private jail. Mama, Papa and my oldest brother Francisco had taken my dear Benjamin to the airport. He headed to meet Juan Carlos in Los Angeles, near Hollywood, home to the famed Chuck Norris and the fearless cowboys of the Wild West. Benjamin and I had loved riding horses. He dreamed of becoming a real cowboy just like in the movies we would always watch. The fact that he was now traveling to this city of dreams gave me some comfort. As I waited for my family to return to me, I paced around the house, and then wandered into the garden haunted by an intolerable loneliness. Papa's words: "You never know when lightning might strike" finally meant something for it had now struck me down. I hoped to be stricken again so that my misery would end. Darkness clouded my mind. I must have slept again, though I have no memory of it, for the next morning I walked to school alone, acting as if sorrow never existed.

13

Shattered Paradise

IT IS NOT long before a child's paradise shatters and innocence vanishes. Adults tend to proceed with their daily business unaware of their children's private worlds. Soon after our last trip to the farm, I put away my water boots. With no significant responsibilities other than attending school, I whimpered about not being able to stay home. The rigidity of the nuns, the predictable order of events and the monotonous rhetoric of my teacher extinguished my desire to go. I endured the long walk there. I took slow steps as the other students passed me by, finding myself the last to enter the gate. At the last toll of the bell, the nuns locked the metal gate with a heavy duty and rusted lock. Posed perfectly in uniformed harmony, we saluted the red and black Sandinista flag along with our

Nicaraguan flag with its triangle representing equality, and sang our national anthem:

Salve a ti Nicaragua en tu suelo,
Ya no ruje la vos del cañon...

Ironically, the anthem claimed that we would no longer hear the sound of the cannon and that the blood of our Nicaraguan brothers would no longer taint our beautiful nation. After this political business, we proceeded in a straight line to the chapel where we listened to our daily mass, and for a few moments no one bullied anyone. No one had more and no one had less. We were all children of the Lord as we praised him with deep repentance and holy incense, but as I looked around the chapel and saw the oversized bloody crucifix of *Jesucristo*, I couldn't help but wonder why God let us hurt Him so badly, and why He was willing to die for us. Always in a straight line, we proceeded to our classrooms and continued to pursue our grueling education. Sit straight. Chin up. Listen carefully, and do not speak unless you're asked to do so. In the morning: unchanged routines, different days. Mathematics: recite the multiplication facts missed. Write twenty times: *I will not climb trees; I will not speak back to the nuns or the teachers.* Writing: No less than readable penmanship earns a 1 score and perfect strokes, punctuation and inspiration earns a 10 score. Reading: read with expression, and don't forget to breathe. Cooking: if you are unable to eat your own dish, then try your recipe again.

We prayed once more, and then finally morning recess arrived again. Recess presented itself as the most exciting activity at school. Securing the first spot in line I ran to the playground, surrounded by trees and a colorful garden, offering my assistance as Nun Elizabeth happily tended to her daily gardening duty. I assisted her in watering the potted flowers and raked the leaves on the ground. While I did this, memories of the farm and the forest brought healing to my soul. When I finished earning points for helping Nun Elizabeth, I quickly lost them by upsetting the Superior Mother.

"Get down, Miss!" She demanded one day as I climbed on a tall and branchy tree located by the fence that overlooked the road. "I'm warning you for the last time," she said, expressing her disgust of an aptitude unworthy of a decent girl in a skirt.

Defiant, and uninterested in being a proper and law-abiding girl, I kept on climbing the tree and sat up high looking at the surroundings of the school and the street. On a fog-free day, looking at the roof of my house, I longed for the school to let out so that I could be there. Nun Elizabeth shook the tree, startling me. I got down quickly and headed back to class. After recess, my day went by faster as I enjoyed art, mannerism and etiquette classes. By then my stomach started to growl. I got into the lunch line with my classmates.

"Today they have creamy cocoa for dessert," a friend announced.

"Do you want to climb the tree with me after we eat?" I asked.

"No! You go," she said, "But I'll be by the gate if you want to come there."

I climbed back up the tree but became bored from the lack of any interesting events in the outside world, so I slipped down to help Nun Elizabeth in the garden instead. Whistling, she pruned flowers slowly with her aged and trembling hands. She smiled at me and pointed to the butterflies that were visiting that morning. The second bell rang, but it went unnoticed by me. I became lost while chasing butterflies in the gardens of the infamous *Colegio Del Sagrado Corazón de Jesus.*

The misty skies, the smell of fresh flowers and the presence of Nun Elizabeth in her subdued servant role brought a strange mixture of feelings to my heart. It was then that I ended up standing against that old metal fence. The smell of the rusted iron suddenly overshadowed the fragrance of flowers and forever turned my childhood dream into an eternal nightmare. Still unaware of the time, I sighted a man dressed in torn civilian clothes across the street at the former home of a family, a home earlier confiscated earlier by the new government and turned into a military base. Walking in a slow and weakened manner, he kept pleading, "Please understand. Please understand."

The soldiers pushed the man using their sharp boots, ignoring his pleas. Then they kicked him to the ground, causing him to gag. I stood frozen. My strong curiosity forced me to stand there as another soldier came and tied his hands behind his back with a rope, turned him around and then covered his eyes with a cloth. Unsure of whether I was daydreaming or not, I remained still and silent. I stood there behind that fence, miraculously silent, as if God's hand had sealed my mouth.

"Move it!" the soldiers shouted. "Move it!" another kicked.

My feet were heavily grounded as I watched the man, who appeared strong and tall, being forced to kneel down. I heard him beg as hard as anyone would be, when one's life hangs on a thread.

"Please, don't kill me. I will collaborate! Please don't kill me. In the name of God, please don't kill me!"

"Please don't kill him," I begged in a choking silence.

Unimpressed, a soldier lifted him up and made him walk to a center location, pushed him down again with his foot and pointed a long rifle at him. I could not decipher his words. They were of the sort of patriotism, something to do with the nation. He then proceeded to shoot him directly in the head.

"Que fuerte venis..." I prayed in my mind, as counseled by Mama in the past. That moment gushed through my body like the blood of the fallen man, as my knees weakened and my tongue froze.

Only my heart pounded as if signaling I was still alive. The silenced sound of the weapon somehow echoed through my ears as they became clogged, and the sight of the man's body losing its power and slipping slowly onto the grass disembodied me. For some reason, this particular dead body had a different impact on me than the ones from the carnage exhibition after the war in town. I couldn't explain why it felt so differently. Perhaps it was because his blood was still warm and it flowed out of his body before my very own eyes from where I stood. Was it the overpowering feeling of impotence that I felt? I do not know.

"Ileana!" Nun Elizabeth exclaimed in a hushed tone, "You are exceedingly late. What in the world is wrong with you child; have you no concept of time?"

Time. What an irony! My mind wondered if she had become oblivious to what had happened or if she only pretended. I stood still and unresponsive with a blank stare and a barren heart. My body had become polluted with thoughts of confusion, incapacity, shame, fear, hatred, anger and even guilt—but I'd done nothing except standing there. The thoughts poisoned my bloodstream, and I felt impotent for witnessing the strange man take in his last breath before my eyes, as I stood there non-existent. I remained heavily silent, despite Nun Elizabeth's shaking. Her voice only resonated in my ears without meaning. My words remained locked for quite some time but later, when my tongue was no longer numb, I asked her if she had witnessed the murder.

"What are you talking about, child?" she asked confused, looking over across the street where I was pointing. "You must be crazy, get back to class. Nothing happened over there."

"I saw…" I cried.

"YOU SAW NOTHING!" She scolded gently but seriously, shoving me behind some bushes.

"Please go back to class now," she pleaded.

"But a man was killed right before my eyes!" I assured her with despair. Nun Elizabeth covered my mouth with her calloused hand; she still smelled of roses and chrysanthemums.

"Please go on, dear," she insisted, "hurry."

I stared at her in disbelief as she kneeled to my level, holding my chin up so that I would look into her eyes. The words that exited her mouth did not make sense to me at that time and made me even angrier. Her image had crumbled before me.

"Listen carefully child, when you get older you will understand that not everything we see is there."

I never cried harder in my life. "Please mother, I just witnessed a man getting killed. It was worse than at the slaughterhouse. His face was covered; he was kicked; he…"

"Silencio!" The elder nun demanded while jolting me into reality. Stern, calm and collective, she stood in front of me and told me words that I would hear again for years to come.

"For your family's sake, child, forget about this madness and go to class. You will have after school detention for wandering about and neglecting your education. If you continue to tell anyone about this, not only will they ignore you, but your family, including you, might suffer the same fate as that man."

"You saw it, too," I confirmed. Her words had confirmed what I had seen and suddenly images of my family being killed like that poor man entered my mind and drove me into despair. I ran to the restroom, locked myself in and cried. Like thunder flooding into my mind, I remembered the story of my brother Juan Carlos's lost love and realized that there was nothing romantic about such an abominable and barbaric act. I wept for my poor brother and the death of Esmeralda, for then I understood his anguish. I also wept for the boy who had been blown up by a grenade and his innocent curiosity that had led him to it like me at that moment. I cried. I cried for neighbors and friends who had lost their land and their precious children and for my innocent school friends who were taken away to fight battles without training. Everything in the world seemed to give a reason for me to cry, and I nearly drowned in my own tears.

After a few minutes of thunder, the Superior Mother came rushing and tried to open the door to the stall I had hid into. She demanded, *Sal de allí inmediatamente,"* knocking on the door with the infamous wooden ruler. Surprisingly, I was no longer afraid of her or the ruler. When I unlocked the door and stepped out, she appeared like an angel in comparison to those soldiers. My appearance must have been overwhelmingly sorrowful for when she saw me the ruler subdued and all she said was, "Come child, everything is going to be all right. Tomorrow will be another day. Here, go on and play with your friends." Knowing that winning over my friends with jacks would be one of my favorite games at school, she handed me a bag with new neon jacks and a bouncy ball. My hands were still shaking as I humbly grabbed the bag of jacks. I headed slowly to my classroom with a confused disgrace, still teary eyes and the feeling of terror still rumbling deep within. I felt numb, nauseated, tired and ultimately, lifeless. Inside the classroom, the still innocent students were engaged in their own respective groups. Some were solving math problems, while others were filling up a graph with the winner of most jacks.

"Come here," a friend called.

Every step I took moved in slow motion. My feet felt unbearably heavy, and my friend's voice felt so distant. I had lost me. These were the slowest steps I ever took in my life, and they took me the longest distance I had ever traveled. I sat down still feeling numb from head to toe, immobile, as life went on for the rest of my classmates. *Señorita Pura* greeted me with her usual harsh tone, but now it did not bother me. Humbly and softly, I apologized for being late. She looked at me in disbelief at my docile behavior and went on to teach as if unaware of what had just happened to me. Everyone was surprised and confused about my strange behavior. Sitting by my friends, quiet as a stone and unable to look at them in the eyes, I proceeded to play while I pretended nothing had happened, bracing myself mentally and emotionally. Shame and anger continued to ripple through me for allowing that poor man to die. My mind was polluted with images of death and millions of harsh questions that would go unanswered. I was afraid my being would corrupt the innocence of my friends with the horrifying scene of the man's head blown open.

"Go back to your seat; we will now take a test," instructed Señorita Pura.

I hunched slightly with the weight of my sadness, forgetting to follow the rule of sitting straight. The old and weathered teacher slammed her wooden ruler on my desk, and threatened to hit me with it if I did not straighten my back immediately. Unable to control myself, I grabbed the ruler as she held it up to my body. While she struggled to keep a hold of it, the ruler broke.

"No one hits me again, not even my own Papa," I challenged.

Indeed, I had learned a lesson that day, one that reminded me that fairness was at times non-existent, and justice was not for all, at least not on the ground I stood on that day. How could it be that a person could take another's life away, at close range, when that person is begging to live? I asked myself numerous times. But more terrifying to me was the gross image of a person taking another's life, and then sitting down to eat lunch on a bench nearby as if the human just killed was only a fly that had been swatted.

My adventurous personality and insatiable curiosity took a long and quiet break. The evil scene disturbed my days and nights. I was even cautious with the people I trusted as the paradise of my childhood had ended abruptly. My life now evolved around a new reality, the type that kept Mama sad, Papa tamed, my brothers distressed and my sisters timid. In a matter of seconds, I awoke to a cruel truth where suddenly the murdered man was not the only victim of terror and destruction. The constant devastation of the forest, the extraction and elimination of many wild creatures, the plants and animals and the overall disintegration of my family had become clear, a shattered paradise of my naive childhood dreams. Innocence no longer appeared to be mine for all I possessed were bedwetting nightmares as I set out to block the feelings that held me prisoner, feelings associated with the rusty smell of blood and the old rusted fence that was built to keep me safe, away from physical harm.

14

A Land Revealed

THE LONG walk home turned into a purgatory. I had a crushing headache, and a strong feeling of nausea, as the blood of the man slowly leaving his body, along with its rusty smell that had even reached my palates, would not leave my mind. That feeling was obsessive. I attempted desperately to focus on the patterns on the road that had worked before when we traveled to Managua. I attempted desperately to block that recently acquired reality but to no avail. The smell and taste of blood, the trembling of that man's body as it ceased to exist corrupted my mind. I could not rid myself of those images. They were beginning to drive my mind into an emotional tunnel I did not wish to enter. And to top my day, I ended up walking home alone after a school detention for not following directions, for being late to class on that atrocious morning and for breaking my bullying teacher's ruler. I felt like the loneliest child in the world and missed my brothers and sisters even more. I wished to share what I had seen, my despairing confusion, my fear and anger, but had no one to share.

As I walked on, the land that saw me grow came to me, and I slowly became detached from my own sorrow. The fog brought a calming mist to my face and temporarily blurred my nightmare and transformed it into a different reality. It was then that I realized that I was not the only victim of destruction. The fog, slowly moving towards the mountains, guided me towards the bald spots that were carving the mountains. At that moment, I stopped to notice the bald spots in the mountains for the first time, even though they had been there all along. I wondered what the mountains had witnessed in their silent dominion over the City of Mist. How many more resistance soldiers had they seen executed and piled up into mountains of human flesh? How many innocent civilians killed in planned accidents or how many minds had gone insane over the witness thereof? I noticed things I never did before. I was no longer blinded by my own childhood innocence.

"Life is not all about fun and games," came to my mind, as I recalled Papa's words that day at the reservoir.

"Anything is possible with God's help," traveled Mama's voice through the wind.

I repeated, everything is possible, everything is possible, and I will forget. As I arrived in town, I was determined to fill my mind with better images. I wanted to love everyone and smile at anyone and anything. I smiled at the store owner in a corner, felt sorry for the crazy woman singing to herself, her gray hair tangled into a maze of lice. I felt compelled to give her a hug and to lie to her about the world getting better. Darkness did not cloud my mind entirely. I became aware of the children who had to work to survive by shining shoes and selling candy, and how they simply enjoyed the life they had by throwing their self-made tops on the ground and betting matches of which would spin the longest.

I questioned if those children, like me, already knew about the kind of world I had just rediscovered. If they did not know yet, I wished for them to continue to enjoy their childhood. That afternoon I felt a mysterious attachment with the common and needy people I did not relate to before. Seeing the humbleness of the people gave me a fragile sense of safety and companionship. I found considerable comfort amongst the *Campesinos*, the peasants carrying crops in their nylon sacks, the down-to-earth people that saw life beyond concealed and unrealistic Country Clubs. The people that traveled the streets that day in my humble town were real. They had learned through the school of life that bravery was found, not in the bearing of a weapon but rather by the outreach to the needy and less fortunate. People proceeded with their business while whistling, singing, and moving to the rhythm brought upon by pieces of wood, pans and seeded maracas. I knew then that the Nicaraguan people were only poor in wealth but not from the lack of spirit. Therefore, I continued on my daily path, the one that would take me back to my garden, animals, and to Mama's daily prayers and enrichment of the soul. As I came closer to home, the last thing I came upon on my long walk was the ominous sight of the few remaining war tanks from the Somoza regime, a reminder of a claimed victory and of the war that had proceeded. I ran into the house looking for Mama, and when I found her, I flung onto her arms and began to cry again. I told her everything that had happened. I cried. I hugged her tight, and shook uncontrollably, but soon became disoriented by Mama's own reaction.

"Vamos a comer," Mama said. "Let's go eat. The Superior Mother called and told me everything, and I was just on my way to pick you up. Why didn't you wait for me?" Mama asked, acting as if all was well. Mama continued trying to act as though she was in control of my shattered world; she did the sign of the cross on my forehead and assured me that everything was going to be all right.

"I made your favorite beef soup and fried plantains for dessert *mi niña*, and Tatiana washed the curtains in your room so that you won't feel sick tonight."

"Mama, I saw a man…" I muttered as if I was talking to Nun Elizabeth again and the soldiers could still hear me.

She ignored me again but the pale look in her face gave her away, and I knew that to Mama what I had encountered today was not a new thing. An unusually long silence followed as we walked to the kitchen. Mama tried to distract me through frivolous jokes but fearsome flashbacks of what I had seen tormented me, along with the words of the nuns and the apparent disbelief of everyone I had told my story. I wondered if I was losing my mind and my dreams had gone out of control. Everyone appeared to go on as usual with his or her own business, except for me. It wasn't just a chicken that had been killed for chicken soup, or a cow for beef stew. Rather, it was the existence of a human being wiped away by merciless spirits. I sat at the table. The sight of the rare red meat on my plate, still bloody, caused me to lose my appetite and gag. Pushing away the table, I ran to my room where I stifled my cries with my face pressed on my pillow; eventually I forced myself to sleep. On that dreadful night, dreams of the forest, my farm, and the animals calmed my spirit while intrusions of evil and the laughter of Satan penetrated my mind, over and over again, until I went into a high fever and I was not able to wake up.

It must have been the sound of Für Elise that intruded into my dreams once more, only this time everything, wild and endangered, moved to the song of "Für Elise," and was lit by bits of moonlight filtered through the dense canopy. A flock of macaws flew down to me and then opened their wings to rise swiftly. Even in the dim light, their flamboyant plumage shimmered like rainbows. A hungry jaguar then moved towards me with silent steps. His eyes locked onto mine, hypnotizing me for a moment with the stare of an audacious flamenco dancer. The intrepid animal prepared to make his kill, but I was undaunted by its predatory goal and pulled away from his power, continuing to dance with open arms, inhaling the sweet fragrance of the wild. My surroundings embraced me. Colorful frogs hopped on the soft carpet of the forest, and howler monkeys swung from vines as the melody rebounded off their cries, scattering leaves. In my sweet dream, I was still the rambunctious child with dangling and soft brown curls, eyes wide open, filled with joy and chronic curiosity, fearless and innocent. The music followed me everywhere, and slowly its melody and the wild cacophony seemed to flow into springs of dark water.

"Bring more water, Tatiana," Mama would instruct.

Mama said that I ran a high fever which lasted a couple of days while my mind went on replaying that horrible scene repeatedly as if punishing me for something awful that I had done. Perhaps I thought, I was being punished for the bad wish for the goose. Eventually, I woke with an even more intense

217

headache than I had on my way home. Although I still felt confused, I also remained somewhat hopeful. Perhaps everything had been just a terrible dream. To my relief, Mama sat next to me. The doctor came and recommended that I see a psychologist. Pacing back and forth, Papa wondered about what I had actually witnessed, worrying that the country was becoming bloodier by the minute. I drifted back to sleep exhausted by a storm of unwanted feelings. I sought nothing more than to erase my memory and re-record the time I had stood by the fence. I pretended I had gone straight to class. I tried to reconstruct my fragile paradise with beautiful, happy memories of my happy childhood. I wanted to play with my toys while warplanes threw bombs at my town. I wanted to ride Lucero through the river and no longer cared if I ended up under his belly. The challenge of the reservoir no longer controlled my nightmares and the stern look of Papa now turned into the most angelical look a human could possibly own. But no matter how hard I tried, I could not reassemble my sweet paradise. The reality of a vindictive and callous world of war had shattered it, the same way it had done to my parents and siblings long ago.

"Let go!" I begged once more, burdened by an unbearable headache.

"Despierta, despierta, todo esta bien," Mama comforted me, reassuring me that everything would be fine. Showered by cold sweat, I rose to see her by my side.

"It was just an unfortunate dream," Mama then said.

"Yes, Mama. It was an awful dream, but it was real."

I spoke to her about what had happened again and asked her why she appeared to ignore me. This time, her face was dull with deep worry. "You are too young to comprehend many things in life," Mama explained. "Life is not always fair, and all we can do is live the best way we can," she added while caressing my forehead. Her soft touch reminded me of the time I lost my dog Ladrón, and how she had made me feel much better.

I know now that she felt my sorrow, and to placate my pain, she allowed me to sleep beside her in her own bed. If there is one thing that still tickles my nose it is the memory of the unforgettable signature smell of Mama's skin. Her pillowcase had magical powers that comforted my heart and calmed my spirits. Mama's arms and her sweet scent never failed to provide a sense of safety found nowhere else. As long as Mama was around, nothing could hurt me. Therefore, from that day on, she guarded whatever innocence remained in me with the fierce claws of a lioness. Inevitably, the time came for me to face my fears and act in my student role once again. I headed back to school, wearing the same uniform as on that unforgettable day. I traveled the same cobblestone road, but not as the same child. I no longer felt like fooling around with my friends or chasing butterflies. I only wished to run away to my beloved cloud forest and be alone with my wild friends. Crossing the road to the heartless military base was the last thing I wanted to do. I wanted to sing wordless songs to show that even though I had been silenced like the beautiful canary of the story, I could still sing within the depth of my soul, for no one could take away my thoughts or feelings. However, every time I attempted to cross, my feet felt like massive weights that prevented me from lifting them into the right direction. No matter how much I tried, I could not get them to cross that path of hell.

A voice that said, *"Buenos Dias, Bella,"* startled me.

It was a soldier from the base across from my school. "Good morning beautiful," he said to me. My stomach churned at his vile act of disrespect. And my mouth clamped shut as if sewn together; I could not open it. I trembled like a leaf in the winter when the wind slaps it in every direction and she hangs onto a brittle branch—barely there. I had heard his squeaky leather boots behind me, and as his footsteps approached closer to me, I wondered if the victim had heard those same footsteps, the same way I had heard them then—only blindfolded and subdued. I managed to run with the force of a hurricane and vomited from the fear of being hunted upon my arrival to school.

I had become an even more frightened child, elusive and obscured at the shattering of my paradise. Trust became impossible, and as a result, I also became afraid to speak. The ease with words I once had deteriorated, for silence became my best friend. But my dreams saved me and kept my blood warm for I knew those moments were just a transient gust of rotten luck. I sheltered my soul for the many endless nights yet to come and only opened it to allow my dreams in. But my dreams wouldn't stay long for I would destroy and duplicate them every night.

As I grew older, I learned that dreams were the dearest secrets of life; they inject hope and can lead to triumph. Therefore, I never gave them up. I became an expert dreamer. I transported myself to the rain and cloud forests whenever there was a window of escape and could not imagine life any other way. I wished for the rain to wash out our tears and rust the chains that made us heave. And at times, I was certain that it was the bright Nicaraguan sun that was causing cataracts in my eyes for I no longer saw Mama smile and my family as a whole at the dinner table. Like ashes in the air, we scattered slowly. In the land where everything is lacking, dreaming is all that is left. Nicaraguans went to school but few found jobs; farmers harvested their crops but rarely feasted. And all I could do was wait fervently for serenades by spirited Nicaraguan Mockingbirds, under the spell of the unreachable moon.

In an effort to ease my turmoil, Mama decorated my room with flowery curtains that turned into a stage at night, entertaining my mind and taking me away from my cruel reality. If I stared long enough the curtains turned into beautiful forests filled with all kinds of wildlife. I would then follow their patterns, as they would allow me to become part of their imaginary existence. Monkeys enticed me to join them on their vines and the ants allowed me to destroy their hills. And as time passed, I slept better, but at random rages of the night, I would wake to that chuckling sound of the rifle and the desolate pleadings of that man. He turned his blurred face to me as I stood behind the rusted gates pointing my fingers in the shape of the gun my Papa had once trained me to use, until he vanished abruptly into the mist.

"Wake up," Mama shouted.

We stared at each other speechless. But eventually Mama resumed her bland routine. And if I had not endured enough, I grew more each day along with my medical calamities but lost significant weight. I had become a body of medical experimentation and shots were given to me day to day without positive results.

"Hold still," ordered the nurse as I squirmed like a worm.

She had come to inject me with vitamin B12 and iron supplement since a previous doctor had killed my red blood cells by inappropriately treating my headaches and coughs, for which I was given endless doses of antibiotics. From day to day, my goal was no longer to escape from school but rather to escape the torture of the needle. Unable to bear one more shot, one day I decided to hide behind a hibiscus tree.

"Find her, she must be hiding," Mama instructed my brother-in-law who happened to be visiting on that day. He found me easily, lifting and holding onto me without much effort. He carried me and held me on his lap as the stunned nurse refused to puncture my body anymore.

"This poor child can't stand to have another shot!" she exclaimed in disbelief as my rear had turned purple and appeared severely bruised.

Exhausted by my condition, Mama decided to try another specialist who finally ended my misery and diagnosed that although the B12 shot had worked for my ravaged nervous system, the cough was merely due to dust allergy, and of course, stress. Therefore, a natural syrup and skunk soup solved my cough problem! It was Papa who set out to look for a skunk and did not return until the skunk was on my platter. I rapidly recovered from my physical ailments, but it was not long before I got into another mess of a bigger magnitude.

"Run, chicken, Run!" is what the chicken should have done.

A few months later, I should have listened to wise Mama when she told me to stay away from the kitchen. We were to have stuffed chicken for dinner, as it was one of Papa's favorite dishes. Tatiana hustled to get the wood for the fire. Mama was busy slaughtering the chicken in the yard. Papa hurried to run his errands, and I had a busy mind.

"Go play!" Mama instructed me.

I hurried to the room to look for Benjamin's toys that he had left me. In a box full of clothes and only a few stray toys, I found his favorite figurine soldiers. Suddenly, I recalled all the happy times we had while playing pretend war in the garden. I hurried to the garden, but as I tried playing with my brother who was no longer with me, images of the people killed by soldiers and the one death I had witnessed overtook me. I played with the toy soldiers, reviving the horrible scene I had experienced. Filled with tears and a pounding heart, I rushed to look for Mama and ended up in the kitchen again. Distracted in my own world, I ran into the boiling pot where Mama had placed the chicken in to remove its feathers. Sudden warmth covered my body from head to toe.

Tatiana and Mama stared at me silently; I returned their stare and then screamed as I ran to the cold water pool to put my burning foot into it. I should have run like a chicken. The boiling pot had fallen onto my left foot. The burning pain was unbearable. The cold water seemed to have temporarily relieved the pain, but when I removed my sock, the skin on my foot came with it and my foot felt cold. Embossed with a beautiful three-degree burn, I still walk with a scar that will forever remind me of my evil dreams. At the point of fainting, Papa rushed me to the local hospital where the doctor cleaned my wound and I screamed with mighty lungs. Ignoring my pleading to stop, the doctor gave me a few shots and bandaged my foot slowly and patiently. And for every wrap, he crafted a whistle.

"She will need crutches for a while, as she cannot set her foot on the ground," he prescribed.

Walking to school took even longer. Every step hurt as much as the memories. Oh, how I wished I could fly like the quetzal, sovereign and beautiful, through the mountains instead of passing through the Path of Death, as I called the path to school. Before I burned my foot, I would literally run to get to school, now I felt punished to endure every single cobblestone and gust of wind shared by everyone that had passed me by. Week after week, a nurse came to my house, only this time to heal my burn. She began by carefully removing the bandage. She asked how I felt, and her soft hands moved slowly through the different stages of painful sanitizing routines.

On the first day, she moistened a large cotton ball with a solution that had no significant effects on my burn. She made her way up to the wound by cleverly cleaning the surrounding areas that hadn't been hurt and then working slowly into the wound. I began to feel her gentle fingers creeping up, and sure enough, I felt the strong burning sensation that gave goose bumps to my entire body. The pain became more aggravating as she deeply cleaned every part of my foot.

"Ouch!" I cried softly as it began to hurt. "Ouch!" I then cried a little louder.

"OUCH!" I screamed as she moved entirely into my wound to do the required "scraping of my foot!" Pulling my foot away, and yelling hysterically, I begged her to stop.

"We are done," she said. "Next time it will be better, I promise!"

I left to go to my room, crying in agony and promising myself never to allow her to touch my foot again. But with each subsequent visit, I was forced to endure the torture again. Each new visit hurt worse than the previous one as she scraped my skin and removed the bandages. I began to dedicate each agony as penitence to the Lord, just like the women who would climb the Tepeyac at my Abuelos' hometown. They did so as an offering to the Lord in order for him to absolve their sins until their knees began to bleed. But one day, I decided that I could no longer take the pain. "No more!" I screamed and finally fainted. When I returned to reality, I could hear the nurse explaining, "She will keep the scar if it doesn't get treated." The scar on my foot remained along with that of my heart. At that moment, the only thing that truly bothered me would be not being able to outrun the nuns, as finally, they had the upper hand. Even with the support of crutches, every step still remained as painful as it had been the first time I had walked to school with them. However, the torture of moving in slow motion as children passed me by was worse.

Enduring that walk was comparable to the *Via Crucis*, a penitentiary walk on the knees that faithful Catholics offer God in order for him to forgive their sins. Humble followers sacrifice themselves by walking on their knees for as long as their bodies can take the pain, sometimes even for miles. By the end of their journey, their knees are scraped and bloody, but their souls are free of sins. Indeed, by the end of my painful offering, after walking slower than a snail, perspiring fear through my pores and experiencing agonizing frustration, I thought that surely I might have been purified—enough to go to heaven and join Amanda. Poor Mama must have been running out of resources, or perhaps she was just trying to exhaust every possible solution. As advised by one of the nuns, the inevitable visit to the psychologist finally took place. Holding my hand, Mama walked me into a ballet studio where his office was located. She let me go out onto the floor with my friends while she met with him. I missed having a normal life, as they seemed to be having.

"If my foot wasn't burned, I could be dancing with my friends," I sighed.

Dr. Wilfrido, appearing sterile and stiff, asked me to come into his office. Pointing to a rigid and unfriendly bed, he said, "I want you to close your eyes and think of a green field." I listened and closed my eyes, but soon opened them to ask, "Why?" Ignoring me, he repeated, "Close your eyes and think of a green field, child."

I closed my eyes again. I could not be forced to imagine without a simple response. Then I asked him why again, until he reworded the question as if I had not understood the first time. "Try thinking of a field full of flowers and birds," he insisted impatiently. Annoyed by the senseless demands of the doctor, and his refusal to hear an explanation, I sat up and explained to him that it was better for me to know why I did things. Irritated, he stood up and opened the door to call Mama. "She will be fine," he said as he walked out of the room.

"Ileana, what am I going to do with you?" Mama complained.

"Definitely," I thought, "the unsympathetic doctor is the one that needed the help."

15

No Return

NO RETURN becomes increasingly familiar in a war-plagued country. Everyone knows when you leave but not when you might return. After surviving rigid elementary school years, my long-awaited day finally arrived. The irony of trying to evade destiny in a small town followed me everywhere I went. Successfully completing my elementary education at El Colegio Del Sagrado Corazón de Jesus, I headed back to the only school of choice, El Colegio La Salle, where suddenly the ghosts of war that had haunted it before appeared less menacing than the live ghosts I had to deal with at the nuns' school.

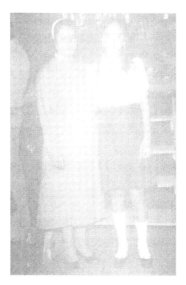

Ileana and the Superior Mother

"Be not afraid of the dead, but rather of those who live," Mama often counseled.

Arriving back at El Colegio La Salle as a young girl was not so terrible after all. Relieved to see many of my childhood friends, including Henry, I armored myself with optimism. Unlike the nuns' school, El Colegio La Salle opened its doors to boys and girls. The beginning of a new life appeared within reach. But the school routine was repetitious, and each day was a replica of the day before. Mandatory Sandinistas' songs followed the daily announcements; flag salutes, prayers—all necessary to boost our daily learning. In a straight, nearly military line, I left to class after recess, often annoyed by one of my best friends. Henry was one of the tallest boys in the class, and I was one of the tallest girls; therefore, in the order of the line, Henry always stood behind me. One day as I walked to class, I felt the sensation of something crawling on my shoulders. Cautiously turning, I felt the object move to the other shoulder. Giggling behind me and holding a leafy stick stood Henry, whose main amusement was to annoy me with bugs.

"Stop!" I demanded, "Leave me alone!"

Slipping and almost tripping on the stairs, he continued to laugh. His immaturity upset me. I made him keenly aware of my plan: never to speak to him again.

"Enough playing," demanded our new teacher, Mr. Castellano. He asked us to take out our writing notebooks.

Serious like priests when offering a mass, we sat at our desks and began to write. Henry loved school and was not about to take any chances that could hinder him from being honored at the end of the year. We must have written for only five minutes when guardsmen came into the class without warning. Mr. Castellano's brown skin turned white as he instructed us to close our notebooks. The men proceeded into the back of the room and walked around staring at the boys.

"You stand up," they ordered Henry.

Startled, Henry dropped his pencil on the ground as I held onto his notebook. Henry walked submissive as they held him by his arm and took him out of the classroom. He looked back at me in shock; his green eyes had become fixated on mine, as if begging for me to tell him that it was just a terrible nightmare. A knot blocked my throat and I simply returned his stare. I felt guilt as I remembered swearing never to talk to him again. Soon after the soldiers exited the classroom, the teacher resumed his position, and then explained to us that Henry would serve as a loyal citizen. Good citizens serve their country well, and that is what he ought to do. Henry stood outside as ordered by the soldiers, like a frightened puppy, side by side with other boys of his height. One by one, the soldiers shoved the new recruits into a camouflaged jeep, like the one that had taken my brothers in the past. Just like that, Henry was done with school, and his pencil and notebook, along with his essay remained at his desk. I would later deliver them to his family.

"Go on and complete your work," the teacher said while sipping on his cup of coffee.

Although the law stated that young men between the ages of 18 and 30 would serve the country in the mountains, the truth was that if they were well grown as Henry was, then they would serve. I was deeply saddened, and terribly frustrated, by the thought of my best friend carrying real weapons and having to make choices between killing, and being killed. The people in our town were merchants, poets, writers, craftsmen and dreamers—not killers. Holding a pencil straight and writing wasn't a viable option for any of us at that moment. We were shaken and scared. Although Henry was the only boy taken that day from our classroom, the other boys were worried, and eventually many broke into tears. The schoolboys knew that their time would arrive, as soon as they became a few more inches taller. They were frightened puppies no matter how much they were encouraged to be brave.

Two months had passed since they took Henry away. Everyone continued his or her daily routines, pretending nothing had changed. I continued to attend daily church celebrations and sang with the choir along with two other friends. On occasions, when my brother Francisco was not too busy, he would take me to the theater to watch a movie. Indulging in sweet treats, soda and forbidden gum, I had what I needed to ensure a pleasant day. For a few hours, the world felt unchanged, but it was not long before we were reminded of our poor conditions.

My brother and I paused to talk about the movie, but became distracted by men with white painted faces dressed in white jumpsuits that would throw buckets tied with a rope from the roof of a building. The buckets were for donations. Seeing these unusual people never failed to intrigue me. The next day I hoped to see Henry sitting by his desk again. Disappointed by the sight of more girls than boys, I continued to pray, read, write, cook and engage in as many activities as were offered. As the teacher continued with the lesson, we sent notes back and forth asking if anyone knew about the boys. One day after school I headed straight home but unusual church bells startled me. I wondered what went on. When I finally arrived, Mama encouraged me to eat and change clothes to attend mass at 4:00 p.m.

"I heard they're bringing Henry back home today," Mama informed me.

I jumped out of my seat with great excitement and headed outside to find Henry. My heart jumped with unimaginable joy. I could not wait to tell him how sorry I was and that he could now speak and play as much as he wished to. But before I could fly out of our house, Mama grabbed my arm and reminded me that we needed to attend church service first.

"Today is Monday," I reminded Mama.

"Yes, any day is suitable for God."

I hurriedly changed my clothes, anxious to get the church service over with. On our way, many people headed towards the town's only cathedral—probably everyone headed the same way, and before we arrived, the bell tolled three times. There was no classical music on that day—just three solemn tolls. I sped my movements; I could not wait to see Henry again. But just before we walked into the gold-adorned cathedral, Mama gently held my arm and pulled me to the side.

"Mi niña," she whispered gently into my ears as she held me close. "I could not find the right words to tell you this, but I cannot let you go inside without knowing."

Something about that way of speaking urged me to run away into the forest and seek the refuge of my wild animal friends. I didn't wish to be there. Whatever it was, I didn't wish to know. I began to walk away as Mama followed and asked me to go back, but on my way, I ran into my friend Erica, who unhesitantly and with watery eyes, soon shared what was to become another bad news in my life.

"Henry will never sit with us in class again. They brought Henry back home. He is there." Erica said as she pointed inside the church.

My throat knotted again, and my chin trembled. In desperation, I ran towards home but stopped halfway as I decided to return in order to prove his death to myself. I walked into the church with heavy steps; my legs could barely support me and also made every moment an unbearable Calvary. Prayers echoed in my ears as voices in a nightmare. Everything seemed so slow, even the tears pouring down his mother's cheeks. The cries of the people, the black clothing and white curtains in the church created the atmosphere of a horror story. Angrily I walked, unable yet to shed a tear, and I could not break free from the thunder that stormed in my heart. I went all the way inside the church. I kept walking on the red runner in the center of the church, ironically representing the Sacred Blood of Jesus Christ. With unknown timidity, I eventually approached the wooden box that rested before the altar and peeked inside, hoping not to see my friend there.

"IT'S NOT HIM!" I told his mother. She then pulled me gently next to her.

"It is him my love," she confirmed sobbing. "Whatever is left of him. Half of his body was brought back this morning. He fell instantly in battle and didn't know what to do. They took him without training, even on how to fire a gun," his mother reproached sorrowfully.

Unable to speak, to believe my eyes, or even to shed a tear, I stood still in disbelief. Memories from my previous nightmares came flashing back, clogging my ears. Henry would not be the first or the last child to encounter such tragic luck. As time passed, more children were killed in combat and accidentally by land mines and grenades left behind in the surrounding fields. The death tolls were high as indicated by the frequent ominous toll of the churches' bells announcing yet another death. I was no longer able to wander around freely in my beautiful surroundings. I spent most of my time in town with friends and family, sheltered by fear and repression. Mama had learned to be strong a long time ago and had passed her strength onto me. Her ways never failed, and she succeeded at raising a child that eventually became resilient to pain, fear and negativity. Attending church services and Bible studies, we made the most out of our lives together. I continued to grow up despite the unforeseen destiny ahead of me.

16

Metamorphosis

THE CLOCK continued its ticking for me, and the day of growth for every young girl came knocking at my door. Papa's little girl had begun to exit her cocoon. Scared to death over what was happening to my body, I ran home to Mama. In kind words, and a little bit too late, Mama explained how remarkable it is to be a woman and how everything about us makes us unique. I did not like feeling unique at all and hid in my house until it was all over. Despite it all, by popular vote, I became one of the nominated candidates for school queen that year. My soon-to-be-king was an unusual boy obsessed with matches. It was a good thing that there was plenty of rainfall; otherwise, he would have burnt the entire town. Carrying a small box of matches in his old worn-out jeans, he used to pretend to burn someone's hair if he didn't like the person. Lucky for me, he seemed to like me. He often winked an eye and blew kisses in the air. His tan skin and his large brown eyes sheltered by exceptionally long lashes appealed to many girls, but Julio was undoubtedly an odd boy. When I asked him why he loved fire so much, he responded by lightning another match and showing me all of the colors in its fire.

"It's like fireworks," he pointed out.

As we became close friends, he shared that he hoped to become a soldier and wished to use real fireworks like the ones that had been dropped by warplanes. We laughed for a while thinking about how he would look if he were to drop fire, as if unaware of the reality such fires brought upon others. He talked and talked about how exciting it had been to be at the evacuation camp and seeing all the lights and flames in the city. It was as he described—unreal.

"I bet you wouldn't be laughing if the fire had burned your own house," I said.

Fixated on his match he said, "It did," and walked away with his match in his hand. Days went by as I busied myself with friends in preparation for the event. The country was busy with a new guerrilla movement guided by proclaimed brave Sandinista women.

"She is almost a woman, *Señora*," the guerrilla women teased Mama when they saw us in the streets.

"No, she is still a child," Mama laughed, nervous from the harassment. "Let her continue her growth."

It turned out that the Women's Movement, as they called it, demanded equal rights for Nicaraguan women that included being drafted into the military. Many women, however, fell under the poetic propaganda sponsored by prominent women poets and writers of Nicaragua, who claimed to carry a weapon as strong as or better than their male comrades. And I often wondered if they truly had the courage to take someone's life as the men did before my eyes, cold-bloodedly? And if so, what could trigger such wombless desire? But I didn't want to know for I hoped they only sought to fulfill their lack of real adventures and detachment from true life. Exhausted by their ignorance, I decided to block their comments and ignore the eminent dangers closing in on my existence. Entertaining myself with my school events, I tried to forget the hurtful things of the past or at least to minimize their effect.

At the same time, Mama busied herself with never-ending errands: house cleaning, organizing cabinets and delivering clothes and toys that we no longer needed to the poor. It was quite unusual to see her with so much energy. Papa had also become involved in this active life and was at home more often. He went to see me sing in the church choir one Sunday and took me to my favorite pastry shop in town. It was the best day that I ever had with him. It was just us, and some annoying people who claimed that I looked like Papa in a skirt.

"Look at her; same identical cleft chin. She is no doubt you in a skirt," they mocked.

Laughing, Papa replied, "She is really pretty then." On the other hand, I did not find it funny. Papa, however, took pride in calling me his daughter, and he especially liked it when people told him that I resembled him. I insisted and pleaded for Papa to buy me a collection of marbles when he stopped by at a friend's miscellaneous store.

"But these are not for you," he said "This is something Benjamin would have liked."

As I was too tired of dealing with only dolls, the enchanting colors of the marbles made it impossible for me to give up trying to get them. Finally, giving in, Papa said, "Fine, but when you see your brother, make sure you share them with him."

"When will I see him again?" I asked curiously.

"Very soon," he added thoughtfully.

"Now, we need to purchase some Cola soda for your Abuelo and some sweets for your Abuela."

"We're going to visit the Abuelos?" I asked incredulously.

"Yes and maybe you can speak to father Odorico as well."

It had been a long time since I had seen my dear Abuelos and could not wait to hug and kiss them and tell them everything that had happened to me. I was excited to see father Odorico as well, for many considered him a close advocate of God for already performing several miraculous deeds. Papa still recalled the moment when after seeing the execution of that soldier, I had asked him to call father Odorico so that he could hear me out and believe what I said. It took him a while to meet my request, and for whatever unknown reasons, Papa was now exhibiting unusually pleasing behaviors. When Papa and I arrived back home, Mama was ready to go to San Rafael Del Norte, the hometown of General Augusto Cesar Sandino's wife, Blanca Aráuz. Mama handed me a handkerchief to cover my nose for the dusty road ahead. The road to San Rafael Del Norte was a rough one. We drove through an all-dirt road, over potholes and slowing down every time there was a bump on the road or soldiers stopped us to inspect our vehicle. As we rode, Mama and Papa talked and I eventually fell asleep, only to be awakened by hush talk and commotion.

"It could have been us," Papa said.

Apparently, the car ahead of us hit a landmine, only a few yards ahead. The military men that had stopped us earlier now rushed to help the victims. We were almost there when Papa turned the car around and began to head back home.

"No, let it be whatever God desires. We could hit one on the way back as well," Mama insisted, wishing to continue the journey to see her parents.

Papa turned around, but we were scared. We drove slowly and as selfish as it might sound, allowed other cars that followed to pass. The feeling of not knowing if we were going to ride over a landmine was a gruesome one. We knew well that every minute that we took a breath was a moment given by God. Upon arrival, Papa acknowledged Mama's comments that God wasn't going to take us to heaven, unless it was our time to go. The town remained the same as when I visited in my younger years. Pine Mountains bordered it and a deep river that ran from north to west crossed it. The river with its unique and pleasant weather accommodates the perfect environment for its verdant flora and extraordinary fauna. It was and still is a small colonial town, humble, uncluttered and picturesque. The streets were narrow as if from the time of cottages, bordered by adobe houses and mostly dirt roads. The San Rafaelinos people are the most humble and warm-spirited people, religiously inclined, and the best Samaritans I have ever encountered. Most lived barely within their means but never failed to offer whatever little they had and that too with smiles worth more than gold. It was the place I wanted to be, a place where everything had intricate flavors. By the time we arrived at my Abuelos' home, my legs were shaking when I exited the car, but at the sight of my Abuelo, I forgot all the hardship we had endured. I ran to my Abuelo and he quickly tickled me with his coarse beard. Abuela followed, kissed both of my cheeks and soon after that braded my hair like hers.

That day we spent the night at my Abuelos' humble home and rejoiced on moments of storytelling while we listened to Abuelo and helped Abuela roll tobacco leaves to make cigars. That moment felt just like old times. My Abuelos brought peace no one else could and helped make everything better. Abuelo told stories, including the story of how Sandino had spared his life. My Abuela told the story, for about the hundredth time, of how she chose to marry my Abuelo against the wishes of her family. And my parents added to the collection of family stories. It was as if they wanted to recall every moment of their lives in an effort to make it part of history. That night I listened to one story after the other. And for the first time, I felt a sense of pride for my family I never knew I had. Since everyone shared his or her stories that night, I figured that I, too, could share my own.

"I saw a man get killed at my school and..." I attempted to tell.

"It's time to go to bed," Mama abruptly interrupted as everyone in the room went quiet.

"I'll put her to bed," my sweet Abuelito offered.

"Abuelo, why won't anyone want to hear my story?" I asked upset.

"It's not good for children to talk about bad things or to think of bad things," Abuelo convinced me.

My sweet Abuelo managed to put me to sleep that night with the longest session of storytelling I had ever enjoyed. That night I had no doubt that we had inherited our attitudes and storytelling attributes from my Abuelos. Anything that came out of their mouths sounded like magic. I had pleasant dreams and awoke the next morning to join a lively town celebration of the Lord of *La Misericordia* who traveled throughout the town on a mule, decorated with flowers and thorns over his forehead. People from all of the surrounding towns and forests came for this celebration and brought their hopes, miracle requests and petitions to the Lord in exchange for penitence of some kind. The streets filled as fervent followers joined the procession. Some followed on their knees while praying. Others were shoeless. The procession passed throughout the entire town until it reached the heavenly cathedral on top of a steep hill. Father Odorico D'Andrea, a wealthy Italian priest who, like Papa and many others became rooted to the soil of Nicaragua, invested his fortune in the development of the town and its monumental church known to be a national monument. Father Odorico also built a temple, now considered being holy, on top of a mountaintop called El Tepeyac, in the shape of a pyramid. El Tepeyac never ceased to amuse. Getting to the top was like getting closer to heaven. Every wide and steep step, if dedicated with a prayer, was said to purify our spirit and just the thought of it, and the fresh air was all I needed to feel the touch of a holy moment.

I could not wait to get closer to Father Odorico. I wanted to tell him all of my troubles, as I knew that he would not ignore me. Seeing him was like seeing a true disciple of God. He wore the same worn-out cassock and old leather sandals. Despite his fortune, the humble priest was solely dedicated to helping the needy. His duty was to help his people even to the point that, if needed, he would offer his own life. It was said that once Father Odorico intervened before a man pinned to the wall, soon to be executed by soldiers. The humble priest put his body in front of the man and told them that if they were going to execute that man before his eyes, then they needed to execute him first. Fearful to be condemned to the eternal fire of hell, the soldiers spared the man's life.

It was a long procession, but life changing. Everyone received holy palm leaves blessed with holy water. Afterwards, Mama, Papa and Abuelos headed towards the monumental church, home of many state-of-the-art Catholic sculptures and incomparable Fresco paintings. Again, stepping into this holy place was as close as we could get to the doors of heaven: stunningly beautiful and peaceful. Regardless of whether a person would be rich or poor, its luxurious decor only reassured that God deserved more than that, and inspired all who walked in that there was hope and that those who believed would benefit in all the richness of the soul possible. The church was the safe heaven to all people. It was an inspiration and a reminder of the beauty of God and life. Father Odorico believed that the house of God deserved the best for all he gave to us.

Upon arrival at the church, the lively priest recited his famous mass, followed by the traditional church tolls and incense. When the father spoke, everyone remained quiet. Eventually the time for the holy Eucharist came, and I proceeded to go ahead. To my surprise, when I approached father Odorico, he stared at me as he placed the holy body of Jesus into my mouth and said that I was okay.

"How does he know that I haven't been okay?" I wondered throughout the rest of the mass.

After mass, everyone retreated to his or her home with a sense of peacefulness, but we waited until everyone had left so that we could speak to the priest. Mama whispered to him and asked for confessions for all of us, including me. I'm sure she whispered to him that I particularly needed to confess. I went last. The rest of my family waited outside as they admired the structure of the church inch by inch. The priest sat next to me and began describing his own childhood. I have to confess that I was in awe at his humble appearance and missed many of the things he said. Other than a priest, I was sure he was also a psychologist for he succeeded at much higher rate than the one Mama had taken me to back at the City of Mist. Before I knew it, I was telling him all about the man that was killed, the goose and Henry. It felt like seconds, and I had told him all about my short-lived life. For the first time, someone listened to me without a single interruption—his face sweet and smiling. He understood what I had seen and felt.

"Who you are is in your heart, and nothing or anyone can ever change that," he explained to me patiently.

He continued to explain the cycle of life and the beauty of death and eternal life for many more minutes and at the end absolved me of all my sins and heavy crosses that apparently I had been carrying. He anointed me with holy water and gave me his final blessing. That was how, for the first time, I felt like a worthy human being, despite my immaturity and young age. The Italian priest of humble demeanor gave me a sense of humanity that would forever remain in my heart. We left San Rafael Del Norte and headed back to City of Mist that afternoon, never to return again.

17

New Beginnings

IN 1987 MAMA instructed Francisca and I to get ready as we were heading to the capital, Managua. We left our town early in the morning as the children were beginning to rush to school and upon our arrival we quickly drove to a place called *La Embajada*, the embassy where, according to Mama, we were to obtain tickets to travel. The lines were far too long, and some people left crying while others smiled.

"*Silencio*, don't say a word, just let me do all the talking," instructed Mama nervously.

Holding Mama's hand, Francisca appeared unusually anxious and remained close to Mama. Praying to go to the window with a pleasant consulate officer, Mama implored to all the saints possible at that moment.

"Next!" a serious official called out. We proceeded quietly to her window.

"Where do you wish to travel?"

"To the United States of America," Mama responded.

"What is the reason?"

"Pleasure."

"With both girls?" she asked, staring at my sister.

"Yes, I have promised them a trip for their good grades," Mama said nervously.

Staring at Mama, my sister and me with penetrating eyes, the woman began stamping our passports. She stamped "APPROVED" to Mama, "APPROVED" to me, and "DENIED" to my sister. Mama felt her womb wither again, just as it had when Amanda passed. She then asked the unyielding woman "Why are you denying her? I'm her mother!" But staring at us without any emotion the woman simply said, "Now you have a valid reason to return."

At that point, Mama had to make a choice. To remain with both of us, risking the threats of the women movement to draft me, or take me out and return for my sister. The choice became clear as we returned home and prepared to travel. My sisters, two brothers and Papa said goodbye as tears fell as though they would flow endlessly. Clinging to Mama, Francisca held onto her arms, refusing to let her go. I clung to Papa begging to make me stay. The thought of leaving my family behind in the hands of unpredictable nightmares broke my heart and shattered what was left of my paradise into microscopic pieces.

Later, as I saddled up on my horse again, I could hear the echoes of the wind and the whispers of the voices of many strange people. It was like a dream, confusing, unorganized and with no pattern. I felt the blood rushing through my head like the first time I rode Lucero as fast as he could run. Suddenly awakened by a strange voice I realized that it was just a daydream.

"Please, take a seat," instructed the flight attendant. "It is time to buckle up; the plane is now ready to depart."

It was only a dream, my last dream of the wind, my horse and I. Mama and I rode a metal horse instead, which flew up in the sky and rode into what would be a new paradise. And as we reached the clouds, my land and my forests faded away, leaving what remained of my family behind. Their tears evaporated into the air, and their pain condensed into the clouds. I knew then my land would soon be flooded again by rain and by more warfare. Meanwhile, my heart flew out way above those clouds swearing never to cry again. The reality before me was that of Mama, a woman armed solely with hope, faith and love. As I sat next to the airplane window, thoughts crowded my mind about the uncertainty of a new life without my forest, my wild friends and my lovely family. Then, reaching inside my pocket for a handkerchief, I felt the note my friend Julio had given me before I left. I took it out and remembered what he had said to me while handing it over to me.

"Please, don't open it until you are gone," he asked while blushing gently. "Let me know what you think upon your return."

Then he shyly walked away. His words confused me. I put the note inside my pocket and left to meet Mama without saying anything, not even goodbye. Standing by the road and waving, he stood there for as long as we could see each other. The tears on his face caused a strange discomfort in my stomach. What is the big deal? I thought. It's just another trip.

Sitting by the window, I finally opened the note and became embarrassed. I protected the note from Mama's eyes and quickly read it, noticing his meticulous penmanship. My tongue became dry and I became unable to speak. I nervously gripped Mama's hand and squeezed it so tight that she asked the flight attendant for assistance. It is human nature to continue somehow. Along the way, the heart goes on as well, as one door opens and another one closes. I missed Papa and all the adventures we could no longer share. I missed how Abuelo would tickle me on my neck with his coarse beard. I even missed Papa's punishment and stubborn drills to toughen me. All of a sudden, the realization of the tremendous loss hit me like a cramp. What happened to my once happy family? What about my childhood innocence? Questions after questions filled my head. Leaning on Mama's shoulders, exhausted, I fell asleep, remembering the last words Papa had said to me. He had embraced me while advising, *"Aspira muy alto! Nunca temas y nunca olvides."* Aim high. Never give up, fear or forget. His words became ingrained in my heart and mind. Looking at Mama and silently promising to take care of her someday, I gave her a kiss and relaxed. Mama and I were indeed to climb a high hill, but I knew better than to give up on the owners of my heart: my beautiful land and people. It was simply the way it should be. During our entire flight, Mama prayed as if hoping to block reality. I grew concerned about her lack of clarity, but filled myself with hopes for a two-way ticket. As hard as I tried to appear tough, random tears escaped from her soul, and at that moment, I could feel the pain she was going through. She had left her land of birth, her beloved children and the love of her life.

Sympathizing with her, feeling the pain of leaving my siblings and friends behind, I could only imagine the inexplicable sacrifice of leaving the man you love, your partner and the owner of your obstinate heart. Amazing is the love of a mother to endure such sacrifice. It was clearly due to her unconditional tolerance towards Papa that her heart still belonged to him.

When we finally landed at Los Angeles Airport, the endless rows of lights I saw through the window reminded me of a new life to come. Mama gripped my hand and lifted me off my seat. *"Mi niña,* it is time to go," she announced. I looked out of the window once more. My childhood memories were rapidly becoming a blur in the high clouds.

"Don't say goodbye. We will always be there for them, and they will always be there for us. They are not dead, yet," she said. From that moment, the courage and deep love Mama portrayed penetrated the deepest part of my heart. I felt nothing but respect for a woman of such character, who sacrificed her life and armed her spirit solely with the weapons of love and hope. Mama made a choice, a painful one, as she left half of her children behind in a country that appeared to have been forgotten by God and the rest of the world. I then wondered if the next paradise would also be shattered. The truth, only the future could tell. "Not even the leaves move without God's will," Mama had always said.

Perhaps I would ride again freely and the memories that shattered young memories will remain just that—memories of a once shattered paradise. Holding hands, we entered a new type of jungle, one with countless lights, cars, people and places. An unknown jungle we would soon explore with dignity and pride, together as a free mother and daughter. Upon exiting the plane to the over-whelming airport, we rode in a friend's car that picked us up and would take us to my brother Benjamin the next day. I rubbed my eyes again to awaken the next day in someone else's home. We were now in one of the most prosperous countries in the world, the United States of America. Everything appeared far, and crowded—and I felt so minute and lonely. I would no longer rise to ride Lucero through whimsical forests, awake to the crow of the rooster and worse yet, I could no longer speak, for everyone that spoke to me in the streets did not comprehend my speech. The following day we headed to a place called the DMV. I needed to acquire an identification card and take a picture in order to attend school and incorporate myself as a good citizen. Mama and my brother's friend then drove us to a building. There were long lines, windows with numbers and crowds of people— perhaps half of the population of where I'd come from.

"Number...!" A woman from behind a counter shouted. But no one responded. "Number...!" she insisted, and again no one responded. My brother's friend then took the number away from my hand and said, "It's you she's calling!" I had waited for someone to call me by my name—Ileana.

18

Window to the World

TWENTY-FOUR years have passed since I left my native land. And it was a splendid morning when it all returned to me, and the hope of spring became the glory of summer. And on that morning, with the slow movement of a three-toed sloth, I looked out my window at the beautiful Southern California landscape that has now become my home. It was the last month of spring, when golden poppies bloomed, and I felt the happiest.

However, nothing remained the same for me on that day. The ordinary transformed once more into endangered species. Each hour's stroke of the clock became a haunting passage of time. And how I wished to rewind the fragments of time, to re-piece the puzzle of our lives together, to bring the dead to life and the sorrows of so many back to innocent smiles and former play. I now know better and recognize that life is priceless and has reasons for being the way it is. No one should cry when alive or even beyond the afterlife, for life is truly a game awaiting our play with rhythmic lyrics and dances of hope.

Nothing ever remains the same, for today we might find ourselves in the abyss of the sea and tomorrow on top of the tallest peak. I'm no longer that troubled little girl; somehow I have learned to adapt in the form of water like Bruce Lee once said. I blend easily within the comfort of my number, the fast pace of traffic and my endless chores at home and work. No one could tell a trace of sorrow in me for I have also learned to smile big. But every now and then when I head out into the busy streets, the smooth asphalt turns into uneven cobblestones, and my eyes see a line of leaf-cutting ants rushing uphill on a winding road. And as I rub my eyes with the palms of my hands to wake me from my new daydream, my imagination has once again taken flight. The ants wear clothing and carry stacks of paper and briefcases; their legs have wheels to help them follow the scent of the green currency all seem to desire. At the top of the hill, at crossroads, anteaters await, their fur covered with well-pressed uniforms; they monitor diligently for ants to break the civil code of uninterrupted patterns. The anteaters pull the ants aside if they fail to conform to the rules and penalize them large amounts of the green currency they carry. But after staring for a while, my ears vibrate at the thunder of an old Corvette revving up, which my dreamy mind transforms into the roar of a hungry jaguar. I cannot wake, don't want to wake. Perhaps I will return again to that land and visit the misty forest and to its fauna and flora, listen to the new stories of those that remain and relive my life of many lives. But perhaps that will be another story and another day.

Acknowledgements

*No accomplishment,
small or large is done alone.*

Special thanks to my husband and best friend Joseph; my two lovely blessings, Abigail and Andre; Mama, Papa, brothers and sisters—without you nothing matters. I love you. My great friend, and at times advisor, Francisco A. Lomelí, you believed in my work since the very beginning, supported, and ultimately pushed it to the next level—with honesty and without any hesitation. A lifetime may not be enough to show my appreciation. Thank you Jim and Marty Dobkins, great friends and formatting advisors. Alethea Eason, my earlier editor and friend, thank you for handling my work ever so delicately. Bruce McAllister, when I first met you at your own book signing, I was inspired and later counseled—your guidance at the beginning of this project and your friendship thereafter is greatly appreciated. A world of thanks to everyone at New Trends Press, you made publishing a joyous adventure. Lastly, to you, the reader, thank you for giving my story a place on your bookshelves. You honor me.

More About the Author

*"My greatest inspiration
is living life to the fullest—however long that
life might be."*

Ileana Araguti

Should you meet Ileana today, you cannot tell of any troubled past, either from her childhood or as an immigrant. She camouflages her past well with joyous laughter. She loves living life to the fullest. Her writings are intended for inspiration and awareness. She strongly believes that any child who has been caught in a war or has been affected by it is a 'war child.'

Ileana's first years of high school were quiet. She took refuge in her "non-existence," as she puts it, amid one of the largest public high schools in Los Angeles, Belmont High. At first she struggled to adapt to her new reality, "her new jungle." But as time passed, she spent most of her time reading and became fascinated with literature. Later in her life she often found herself writing notes to express her emotions, only to throw them in the trash later. Her father stopped paying her mother any child support, as he felt abandoned. Therefore, together with her mother, she endured years of struggle and poverty as most U.S. immigrants do. Nonetheless, she managed to eventually put herself through college and acquired a Bachelor's Degree in the Arts at the University of California, Riverside, and later two more Master Degrees.

Ileana is currently an educator, a writer, wife and a mother of a son and a daughter. She enjoys traveling with her family and resides in Southern California. Ileana returned to visit her native country of Nicaragua twenty-one years later. Upon her return, she rediscovered a totally different country from the one she left behind. It was then that she decided to write with the hope of bringing awareness about the devastating effects of war in children, and ultimately about her beloved and vanishing rain and cloud forests.

Forthcoming work:

A Pedal Away, a novel (Fall 2013)

Visit her website and blog for news on her upcoming work or to simply chat about life.

Website: www.ileanaaraguti.com

Blog: www.ileana4earth.blogspot.com

Twitter and Facebook!